In a small room, in a suburb of London, four men sat drinking. After a while, an argument started over the reckoning. There was a scuffle. Knives flashed. When the panting and the cursing subsided, one man lay dead upon the floor, a dagger in his brain. The time was 1593. The place: Deptford, England. The murdered man: England's greatest poet-dramatist, Christopher Marlowe. The result: a quick, quiet, inquest, with the murderer pardoned on a plea of self-defense.

Now, almost four hundred years later, Calvin Hoffman unravels for us the tangled skein of the greatest imposture ever practiced. Marlowe was not murdered. Indeed, the murder was a put-up job; a real-life play, staged for the benefit of the authorities. Its purpose: to spirit away Marlowe, whose atheistic sentiments, and general mode of living, were driving him to the stake.

THE MURDER OF THE MAN WHO WAS

'Shakespeare'

CALVIN HOFFMAN

THE MURDER OF THE MAN WHO WAS

'Shakespeare'

JULIAN MESSNER, INC.

New York

Published by Julian Messner, Inc.
8 West 40th Street, New York 18.
Copyright 1955 by Calvin Hoffman
Printed in the United States of America

Published simultaneously in Canada by the
Copp Clark Company, Ltd.

First printing, May, 1955

5391

.. TO ROSE ..
. THE . ONLY . INSPIRER . OF .
. THESE . ENSUING . PAGES .

WHEN I first began my researches—more than nineteen years ago—into the problem of Shakespeare authorship, I had no wish to add my contribution to a literary recreation which, over the years, had acquired a slightly bar-sinister cast. For many, many years theories on whether or not Shakespeare wrote the plays that bear his name have issued thick and fast from the brains of diverse literary authorities, each of whom brought forth his own special candidate. However, all were united in their disunity by a certain conviction that *something* was wrong with the premise that William Shakespeare was the author of the Works attributed to him.

Before I began my investigation, which finally led to the publication of this book, I was convinced—like most other people—that William Shakespeare was the author of the most magnificent English dramatic prose ever written, and certainly the most magnificent poetry.

Nineteen years later my feelings toward the qualities of this writing have not changed; they are magnificent.

Only, William Shakespeare of Stratford on Avon never wrote the plays and poems.

For almost two decades I pursued a literary will-o'-the-wisp that gave me no rest. My investigations took me to England, France, Denmark, and Germany. I roamed through graveyards, I crawled into dusty tombs, I shivered in the dampness of veritable archives, and in the musty atmosphere of libraries whose book-lined shelves had remained undisturbed for centuries. Across my mind's eye there still unreels the endless procession of ancient houses, decaying churches, and old universities which I patiently investigated as an unofficial detective in a murder mystery that rivals any Sir Arthur Conan Doyle ever wrote. I uncovered a real-life literary "thriller," complete with murder, brawls, duels, and normal and abnormal sexuality. A violent, crimson-colored pattern unfolded itself, with England as the background and the splendidly barbaric Elizabethan era as the setting.

As the clues came thick and fast, I found the load of my inquiry often too heavy to bear. I earnestly prayed that sufficient reason might be found to abandon my search, since it gradually consumed most of my thinking hours, to the sacrifice of more worldly rewards.

The deeper I entangled myself in the evidence at hand, the more carefully I examined the few facts, the welter of conjecture that moldily surrounded the life of William Shakespeare, the more I became convinced, almost against my will, that my search could never be dismissed or ignored as just another unorthodox theory.

Finally, there grew to dominate my days and dreams an imposture unbelievable in magnitude. History had rarely recorded its like. Here was a masquerade that created heartbreak, doomed its protagonist to eternal anonymity, while strait-jacketing him into everlasting silence.

That the life of the man responsible for the greatest poetry and the greatest dramatic prose and verse in the history of the English language should have been deliberately shrouded in anonymity during the most creative years of his life, that he might have been fated so to remain forever is nightmarish to contemplate.

Certainly no character the author envisioned on paper ever matched the depth of his own tragedy. If ever a hell was created for a writer, it was this. Here was a man of surpassing genius, rich with words and overflowing with creative fervor, doomed to live his life watching another gain the plaudits, the rewards, and the fame that rightfully belonged to him. And all he could do was to continue to write and to suffer in silence.

Stifled by a suffocating gag, his soul galled with disappointment, he must have departed life an embittered, lacerated man.

And yet, while living under this weight of spiritual and mental hell, he never ceased to write. A torrent of exquisite poetry, sublime plays, and unmatched ideas endlessly poured from his pen.

There are certain people who have often commented upon the wasteful voyagings made in tracking down the genuine author of the plays and poems known as William Shakespeare's. They care not, they say, who wrote them. The kernel of their arguments is that the subject of authorship is not of the slightest importance.

In the last analysis, these same individuals assert that the glorious plays and poems exist for the world to enjoy. "What difference does it make *who* wrote them?" they ask.

They are entitled to their point. But it does not delve to the core of the matter. To understand Shakespeare, and what he has written, it is not sufficient merely to read him. Here is a writer who not only requires our gravest attention but, as is the case with all extraordinary artists, commands our deepest reverence. It is not enough to use one's head to read Shakespeare. One must also offer one's heart. He brooks no half-love. No page browsers can woo him successfully. And if, in all earnestness, you grow to love and reverence his works you cannot assume an attitude of indifference toward the Man himself—toward the suffering soul who haunts, now visibly, now invisibly, the length and breadth of the Works.

The personality of the author of the plays and poems known as Shakespeare's is inescapably linked to the creations themselves. The bond is so tight, the weld so joined and perfect, that it is nonsense to believe one can, at the same time, admire merely what has been written and ignore the author.

Samuel Butler affirmed the truth of this when he stated: "A great portrait is always more a portrait of the painter, than of the painted."

What manner of man was it who painted titanic word pictures couched in sublimest sorrow and beauty? The man who wrote:

> To-morrow, and to-morrow, and to-morrow,
>   Creeps in this petty pace from day to day
> To the last syllable of recorded time;
>   And all our yesterdays have lighted fools
> The way to dusty death. Out, out, brief candle!
>   Life's but a walking shadow, a poor player
>   That struts and frets his hour upon the stage
>   And then is heard no more. It is a tale
>   Told by an idiot, full of sound and fury,
>   Signifying nothing.

Who was this man? The question is important. The answer is strange, and wonderful.

Tracking down the identity of our author is not only necessary, but mandatory. It is a command I have not dared disobey.

"What difference does it make who wrote the plays?" There is, I believe, no question of "difference." Rather, there is a question of better understanding one of the unusual minds of the world.

The results of my work are not those of which I had dreamed. They are simply, and often incredibly, the truth.

If there is in the story I have to tell a touch of the academic grandeur inherent in any literary effort which, no matter how fleetingly, touches upon the life and the writings of the man we know as Shakespeare, there is also, as a dramatic counterbalance, an unfolding of the weirdest cloak-and-dagger tale ever conceived.

Crime, guilt, fraud, and exile; hate, deceit, murder, and despair. All these luridities have woven themselves into a shroud that, until today, hid the identity of the world's most renowned writer.

That the most eulogized author of the past half-millennium should have been forced to live his high-noon hours a pariah in his native land; that when he should have been enjoying the fruits of his prodigious labors he was, instead, living in perpetual exile; walking forbidden coasts in silence and in fear; perhaps slipping his completed manuscripts under a bolted door; running forever like a thief in the night. All these truths introduce into the story the element of irony. There are, and were indeed, "more things in heaven and earth . . . than are dreamt of in your philosophy."

Disbelief that William Shakespeare wrote the plays and poems attributed to him was inevitable. The wonder is that the awakening came so late. More than two hundred fifty years rolled by before a skeptic's voice was raised.

One hundred years ago the first doubts began to make themselves heard. The meager record of Shakespeare's literary life; the lack of any personal reputation among his literary contemporaries; the bankrupt evidence of any formally acquired education which (considering the time in which he wrote) he *must* have had to write as he did; his emergence with incredible suddenness as a writer in his thirtieth year—oddly late for a poet of the Elizabethan era to have first flowered; the prosaic events of his unrecorded literary life, which are all we definitely know about him—these and many other reasons were stirring the first yeast of doubt in the minds of thinking men.

The first dissenters favored Francis Bacon as the author of the Shakespeare plays and poems. Following the Baconians, other candidates were brought forth. The Earls of Oxford,

Rutland, Southampton, and Derby were among the perennials. The contention was that only those born into the nobility or associated with it could have written the noble thoughts and described the aristocratic characters in the plays.

Though the choices offered are symptomatic of an ability to renounce Shakespeare in general rather than a thoughtful selection of the right condidate, I applaud these "doubters" nevertheless. They have managed to unshackle themselves from the handcuffs of a declining tradition. They form part of the crusade to win for the rightful author his merited due.

But the brave and articulate individuals who have in books or pamphlets championed other men as author of the plays and poems are not alone in rejecting William Shakespeare as author. An impressive array of unbelievers—none of whom has necessarily written a book on the subject or presented a candidate for the authorship—have made known their sentiments. All meet in the belief that Shakespeare just cannot be accepted as the author of the works credited to him.

Such men as Nathaniel Hawthorne, Lord Palmerston, Walt Whitman, Sir George Greenwood, Mark Twain, Prince Bismarck, Oliver Wendell Holmes, Sigmund Freud, John Bright, Henry James, Lord Broughton, Ralph Waldo Emerson, Lord Penzance, John Greenleaf Whittier, Dr. W. H. Furness; and Charles Dickens, who declared: "The life of William Shakespeare is a fine mystery, and I tremble every day lest something should turn up."

What is the significance of these doubts? The stature of the members of the Shakespeare revolutionaries speaks for itself. They cannot be dismissed as "clowns" or "cranks" or "crackpots." Scholars, students, critics, and commentators have contributed to the Shakespeare study—and are numbered among the unbelievers. Even though their theories as to *who* wrote Shakespeare's plays appear untenable, yet their unified disavowal of Shakespeare's authorship—the major premise behind all their conclusions—cannot be lightly disregarded. These men are not irresponsible eccentrics. But, then, who did write the plays, and the poems?

To begin with, a successful candidate must fulfill certain conditions. Before superimposing on Shakespeare's image the image of another—a nameless one—and then identifying that superimposition, certain qualities must be found, examined, and proved. The supporters of the faceless candidate must be able to produce reasons relentless and inevitable, or else join the ranks of Francis Bacon, Oxfordites, and other contenders. Until such a nominee is presented, capable of passing the most stringent critical tests known to logic and literature, denial of Shakespeare's authorship, while intriguing, stimulating, and often conclusive, does not deserve acceptance. A god cannot fall unless another god arises.

In the following pages I present for your consideration a poet-dramatist whose genius, education, known literary output, and accomplishments prove to my mind that it was impossible for anyone else to have written the works attributed to William Shakespeare.

For one of the first times the name of this poet-dramatist is put forth in the pages of a book as the author of Shakespeare's works.* Seventeen years of effort and research have

*A) It was not until at least 12 years had elapsed in my research that I learned of the following:

In 1895, W. G. Zeigler, in a cinematic "thriller," fictionalized the tale of Marlowe's "murder" by *reversing,* of all things, the documented facts. Instead of Francis Frazer (Ingram Frizer) slaying Marlowe, Frazer, in turn, is stabbed to death by Christopher Marlowe, after he, Frazer, discovers Marlowe trysting with his faithless wife in the bedroom of his home.

Ziegler's scenario-novel then imagines Marlowe having been slain, *in 1598,* by the dramatist Ben Jonson!

The whole tale is compounded of the purest fiction and fantasy.

B) In 1923, one Archie Webster, in a terse six-page magazine piece, believed that Marlowe had written the Sonnets.

C) In 1931, Gilbert Slater, in his "Seven Shakespeares," advanced a theory that not one, but *seven* writers wrote the works of Shakespeare. These were: Francis Bacon, The Earl of Oxford, Sir Walter Raleigh, The Earl of Derby, Christopher Marlowe, Lady Pembroke, and the Earl of Rutland.

Slater laid greatest emphasis for authorship on Oxford. Marlowe, he felt, was employed by the other six to merely supply the technique of play construction for them.

buttressed, and made secure, this writer's claim to title. I present the name confidently. For, once the pieces of the literary puzzle have been put together and the complete picture studied with critical eye, it is almost with a sense of anticlimax that Christopher Marlowe, duelist, scapegrace, genius, and poet, stands gloriously accused.

In the winter of 1936 I traveled to the south shore of eastern Long Island, where, in the quiet, I hoped to finish some writing. At first everything went well. For two weeks I wrote confidently, and without cease. Then one morning I awoke feeling that the spell had been broken. I couldn't get on with my work. There is nothing on earth more unhappy than a writer who cannot write. Every morning I sat down in front of a miserably blank sheet of paper and lit my first cigarette. Two hours later there were fifteen cigarettes in the ashtray to the right of my typewriter and the paper was still blank.

After three days of this mocking misery I finally went to the local library, where I borrowed books of most Elizabethan dramatists available. I carried home with me the works of Kyd, Greene, Lyly, Marlowe, and Jonson. I concluded that if I couldn't write I might as well read.

For more than a month I did little else. And of all the Elizabethan plays, I came to know and like those of Christopher Marlowe the best. At all times there seemed to hang over his works an atmosphere of déjà-vu—a nagging, compelling memory that disturbed me as I reread *Tamburlaine, Dr. Faustus,* and *The Jew of Malta.*

I began to jot down phrases, expressions, and lines from Marlowe, and similar phrases, expressions, and lines I recalled from Shakespeare. Placed side by side, these quotes formed the first clue to what was to develop into a gigantic literary jigsaw puzzle, which would occupy me for many years to come.

Later I checked my memory of Shakespeare's quotations

with the text of his plays. I found they squared with those of Marlowe's. An example:

Marlowe's *Tamburlaine:*
> Holla, ye pampered Jades of Asia.
> What, can ye draw but twenty miles a day. . . .

Shakespeare's *Henry IV* (Part II):
> And hollow pampered jades of Asia,
> Which cannot go but thirty miles a day.

Marlowe's *Dr. Faustus* (conjuring Helen of Troy):
> Was this the face that launched a thousand ships?

Shakespeare's *Troilus and Cressida*
> (referring to Helen of Troy):
> . . . She is a pearl,
> Whose price hath launched above a thousand ships.

After a while I realized that what I had done was to extract stylistic similarities, known as parallelisms, from the works of the two authors. The number of these parallelisms grew, and my interest grew along with them. I reread most of the Shakespeare plays. With renewed vigor I found myself startled by the astonishing affinity that Shakespeare had for Marlowe, and Marlowe for Shakespeare. Not only was this affinity one of style, but every facet, every nuance of the dramatic and creative mechanisms in their works seemed incredibly harmonious. Both dramatists created the same emotional, intellectual situations for their characters; more often than not, they were psychologically identical.

It seemed as though versification, vocabulary, imagery, and allusion stemmed from the same psychic root.

Of course, the two poets were contemporaries. Perhaps, I thought, I was overeager; and what I had begun to read between the lines of my Oxford Shakespeare was the result of my own imagination. I reread Kyd, Greene, and Peele, scrupulously setting their lines against Shakespeare's as I had previously done with Marlowe. Quite unconsciously, I was performing a literary "control" experiment.

The results were unexpected. Shakespeare's whole style and treatment differed radically from that of these other playwrights; so did Marlowe's. I found that Marlowe and Shakespeare stylistically agreed with each other in the same inverse proportion as they disagreed with their dramatic contemporaries.

I reread the works of both dramatists. Marlowe's *Edward II, Hero and Leander, Dido, Queen of Carthage,* and Shakespeare's *Timon of Athens, Two Gentlemen of Verona,* and *Cymbeline* engaged me. Thematically, the works were poles apart. Yet the medley disclosed further evidence of a literary relationship between Marlowe and Shakespeare so close, so united that it seemed to me to be almost a blood relationship.

I began to draw parallelisms again. After a while I had collected an enormous number. And it was time for me to leave Long Island.

During all this time my knowledge of the lives of Shakespeare and Marlowe amounted to no more, and no less, than that of the average, reasonably informed person. I accepted the usual academic and textual pronouncements literally.

William Shakespeare died a respectable Stratford on Avon death at the age of 52.

Christopher Marlowe, by contrast, died in a tavern brawl at Deptford at the age of 29—when he was stabbed, murdered in a quarrel over either a wench or an ale bill.

These were statements found in books. I had never questioned them in any way.

The last night before my departure I spent tossing restlessly from side to side. It was one of those euphemistically named "white" nights, which are, in reality, black as pitch; a foretaste of hell, for any tense or nervous person who is liable to brood progressively about loss of rest. Instead of black sheep, I counted parallelisms. And around three o'clock in the morning, with the waves of the ocean moaning outside my window, I began to brood over Marlowe's death. And sometime during that quiet period I asked myself a question: "Was the report of Marlowe's assassination true?"

I don't know quite why, but I felt intuitively that somehow it was not. A small doubt persisted. It was to grow with boom-food rapidity during the months and the years to follow. I determined to seek confirmation of Marlowe's murder; solid, incontrovertible evidence that he had truly died as reported.

That was the beginning of a nineteen-year search for the needle of truth in a haystack of literary conjecture that had been piling up for centuries. And at the end of that time I was ready to prove, beyond any reasonable doubt, that every single play and poem we have been led to believe was written by William Shakespeare had been written by Christopher Marlowe—a poet-dramatist who had outlived his own death, in a most "strange and marvellous fashion."

Let me emphasize here that it was *not* by first denying Shakespeare that my theory came into being. It was the growing conviction that no one *but* Christopher Marlowe could have written the works of Shakespeare.

In spite of doubts, in spite of feeling that I was tilting at the windmills of established authority, I could not help but think that the poet who had written:

> I . . . hold there is no sin but ignorance.
> (*The Jew of Malta*)

had written:

> I say there is no darkness but ignorance.
> (*Twelfth Night*)

That the poet who wrote:

> Weep not for Mortimer
> That scorns the world, and, as a traveller

> Goes to discover countries yet unknown.
> (*Edward II*)

had also written:

> The undiscovered country from whose bourn
> No traveller returns.
>
> (*Hamlet*)

These were but two of a multitude of similar parallelisms. There were other reasons, too. One of them came from Sir Edmund Kerchever Chambers, a knowledgeable Shakespeare authority. Thus, Sir Edmund, in his biography of William Shakespeare:

> The percipience of style is a very real quality. It had its origin in the same natural feeling for the value of words and the rise and fall of rhythm, which is the starting point of literary expression itself; it may be trained, half unconsciously, through reading and reflection and comparison, into a valuable instrument of criticism. A quasi-intuitive sense is developed.

And further:

> A writer forms his own rhetorical habits in the building of lines and the linking of line to line, in the use of exclamation, antithesis, iteration and cumulation; in the balance of noun against noun and verb against verb. A writer has his own small mannerisms of locution, his recurrent catch-phrases. . . . These are the most characteristic because they become unconscious and are often, at first sight, unnoticeable. . . . Naturally each writer has his individual range of thought, of dramatic situations, of imagery, of allusion, or vocabulary.

Sir Edmund confirmed the value of my work—the weeding out of parallelisms between the works of Marlowe and Shakespeare on the basis of "the starting point of literary expression itself."

But no matter how I might be cheered by this helping hand (unconscious or otherwise) of authority, there were other factors to consider. Marlowe's homicide at the age of

29—a matter of historical record—had cut him off at an age when he could not possibly have written the bulk of the Shakespeare Canon.

And yet—and yet—it must be Marlowe!

THE MURDER OF THE MAN WHO WAS

'Shakespeare'

1

FOR two hundred years Elizabethan scholars have agreed that of all Shakespeare's contemporaries the poet-dramatist Christopher Marlowe exerted the profoundest literary influence over the poet-dramatist William Shakespeare. According to scholars, Shakespeare carried through to its utmost limits the literary trend that Marlowe established and later concretized in such plays as *The Jew of Malta* and *Tamburlaine*. Surely these scholars, involved as most of them were in the minutiae of the Shakespeare Canon—men who could write whole, long books about a single character in one play—could have exhibited more than perfunctory interest in the similarities between the two men—both extraordinary writers, both carrying on their shoulders almost the entire burden of Elizabethan literature.

No two events in the history of literature have passed so strangely unobserved as the fact that within four months after Marlowe was murdered Shakespeare emerged, full grown from the head of Jove, as it were, as England's greatest playwright. I therefore begin my case with the following observations:

Marlowe was in his thirtieth year when he was murdered at Deptford, a village across the Thames, on May 30, 1593.

Shakespeare was in his thirtieth year when he burst upon

3

the world as a writer—four months after Marlowe's murder —in September, 1593.*

Shakespeare's first literary work was a poem, *Venus and Adonis*, which was registered with the Stationers Company (an Elizabethan version of our copyright office) anonymously, April 18, 1593. The name "William Shakespeare" appears at the end of an unauthorized dedication to the Earl of Southampton. It is not imprinted on the title page of the book.

Before assessing these facts, it seems reasonable to inquire into Shakespeare's life prior to his sudden emergence as a playwright, which occurred after the slaying of Christopher Marlowe. Similarly, we will cast a glance (a more informed one, let me say) into Marlowe's life, before his assassination.

To begin with . . . Shakespeare.

The results of exhaustive examination, of both private and public archives for three hundred years, have yielded the following three facts—which represent, in their entirety, everything that anyone knows for certain about William Shakespeare up to the age of 30; an age which in Elizabethan times was that of a mature man who should, by all rights, have already made his mark in the world.

Baptism in Stratford on Avon, on April 26, 1564
Marriage to Anne Hathaway in 1582, aged 18
Fatherhood of three children up to February 1585, age 21

This is all that is known of William Shakespeare, up to the publication of *Venus and Adonis*—the first of a series of works, epic in conception and in execution.

What, then, of the interlude between February 1585 and September 1593? Those nine years should normally have been

* The first time the name "William Shakespeare" appeared in print was in a poem "Venus and Adonis," published on September 22, 1593. In an extant diary, kept by one named *Reynolds*, "Venus and Adonis" is mentioned as having come off the press on that date. See Leslie Hotson's *"Shakespeare's Sonnets Dated."* Hotson accepts September 22, 1593, as the date of publication for "Venus and Adonis."

the most creative, the most vigorous of Shakespeare's life. Between the ages of 21 and 30 the Elizabethan man reached his middle-age prime. Surely, this period was the time for trial and error, for those fumbling attempts to poetize which are so much a part of any artist's growth.

During those years William Shakespeare was never referred to by anyone, personally or professionally. Other writers of the times spoke of and discussed each other. No one, however, spoke of William Shakespeare; no one discussed his attempts to write, or what he had written. It is as though prior to 1593 Shakespeare was nonexistent as an established playwright.

Except, of course, for those three slender facts: birth, marriage, fatherhood. These alone stand between Shakespeare and total oblivion up to his thirtieth year, when he first appeared as an author, four months after the murder of Christopher Marlowe.

It has been said, in academic Shakespearean biographies, that "we know more of the life of Shakespeare than we do of any of his contemporaries." This is nonsense if it refers to his first thirty years. If we know so much about the man, how explain the knowledge of only three facts about his life up to 1593, when he had already lived the best part of a man's life? During this time we know only of his baptism, marriage, fatherhood.

The truth is, we know more of the literary life of practically every other contemporary writer than we do of Shakespeare. More personal wisps survive the literary lives of Lodge, Peele, Greene, Kyd, Sidney, Nash, and Christopher Marlowe than the first thirty years of Shakespeare's life on earth. Professor F. P. Wilson, a traditional and orthodox scholar, tells us: "We know more [i.e., the literary life] of Marlowe's 29 years than about Shakespeare's 52 years."

When a man approached his thirtieth year in Elizabethan England he had passed over the threshold of middle age. The life expectancy of the average man during these times was (to be liberal) 40. Both Marlowe and Shakespeare were well in their middle-aged prime during the year of 1593. They could look forward to ten more years of life (if they were lucky; if the plague did not strike them down; if they were not killed in duels, or starved to death; or developed pneumonia; or any of the other diseases or misfortunes that struck down Elizabethan man).

Now, it is obvious that no writer, especially one of Shakespeare's extraordinary stature, could appear upon the contemporary scene with no preparation whatsoever and start composing some of the greatest English prose and poetry ever written. Somewhere in his past there must have been schools and teachers, books and learning. There must have been influences at work to form the man, and through the man, the Works. Such nourishment is external; William Shakespeare could not, for example, have spontaneously acquired the enormous vocabulary and vast book knowledge that his plays brilliantly reveal. He must have had either formal schooling, formidable schooling, or have educated himself. A writer, more than any other artist, is the product of an educational process. It is possible to be an untutored artist; a painter or a sculptor can occasionally, through his native genius, create beauty with no inspiration other than his inner self. The ability to write, to use words, can never be spontaneous in origin. It is the end product of external knowledge, plus studious application. As far as we know, Shakespeare never received a formal education. He is not known to have even attended grammar school. Any statement to the contrary is based on wishful thinking.

Compulsory education was unknown. Secondary schools did not exist. We know, concretely, that Shakespeare never attended a university. There were only two institutions of higher learning in Renaissance England—Oxford and Cambridge—and Shakespeare attended neither.

6

Therefore, we know absolutely nothing of Shakespeare's schooling.

Might he not have been self-educated? He could have acquired an education through reading. Many eminent men have done so. But William Shakespeare lived four centuries ago; at a time when the bulk of the Elizabethans were illiterate—when it was an accomplishment to be able to write one's name; when only the affluent and the few could read at all. The mass of the people had been but recently disenchained from the intellectual manacles of the Middle Ages. There were no public libraries, no private endowments, no lending stalls, no book-mobiles. There were no dictionaries, no encyclopedias, and no English grammars.

The printing press had come into being less than 135 years before Shakespeare's boyhood. Books were laboriously printed and bound by hand. The public supply of books, therefore, was meager. As for the two universities, each with an enrollment of over a thousand students, each had but a few hundred books in its library. A good many of these books were actually chained to desks so that pupils could not borrow them. Reading access to these volumes (for students only) was permitted only during morning and afternoon hours, and required a fee. As for strangers, they were not allowed to trespass on the university ground. In truth, books and free access to books were an impossibility for the average Elizabethan.

Further, the cost of the few translated and untranslated volumes that circulated mostly in the cities was beyond the means of most men. William Shakespeare, son of a Stratford tradesman, could hardly have afforded to travel to London to purchase books, especially during the poverty-stricken years of his adolescence and early manhood.

Married at 18—father of three children at 21—would a life as full of responsibility as his allow for the hours of solitude necessary for "self-education"?

7

We are asked to believe that this young man, living in a village of at most 2,000 people, lacking money, time and opportunity for self-education, never recorded even as an elementary school student, could suddenly, at the age of 30, begin to write exquisite verse and highly sophisticated drama.

It is more reasonable to state that William Shakespeare on the basis of known facts could not have acquired the self-education necessary to construct a complex sentence.

There is no evidence of any sort that believers in William Shakespeare's authorship can produce that will meet one of the two requirements for any author: education, or self-education through reading. And until that evidence is forthcoming, it is fair to state that William Shakespeare was not educated enough by far to have written the Works attributed to him.

To be just, I should produce the evidence brought forth by the Shakespearean advocates. Here are some of their theories on William Shakespeare's education:

(1) It has seriously been stated by Shakespearean zealots that the sources of Shakespeare's education must not be questioned, since "genius," *ipso facto*, requires no explanation; that Shakespeare was beyond the necessity of learning, of all educative preparation.

Inherent in this belief is the absurd notion that the formal acquaintance with the works of Socrates, Sophocles, Virgil, Seneca, Ovid, Plautus, Lucan, and Pliny; with Latin, Greek, French, and Italian; with the arts of grammar, medicine, poetics, philosophy, divinity, astronomy, versification, law, and horticulture, had dropped "as the gentle rain from heaven" upon the man from Stratford.

This knowledge must have been garnered through some external means. Shakespeare's sensitivity argues not only for general knowledge, but also for a systematized knowledge of

8

the intellectual world. No wonder Samuel Taylor Coleridge, in this connection, tells us:

> Ask your own hearts, ask your own common sense, to conceive the possibility of the author of the plays being the anomalous, the wild, the irregular genius of our daily criticism. What! Are we to have miracles in sport? Does God choose idiots by whom to convey divine truths to man?

The miracle of Shakespeare's education, or self-education, is an impossible miracle. It argues only the limitations of those who incline to such a possibility.

(2) Another school of Shakespearean orthodoxy indulges in a wishful thinking perhaps more disciplined—but wishful thinking nonetheless. These good gentlemen claim that the Stratford boy secured his education through the paternal benevolence of a patron (unnamed), who recognized his genius in the making; took him home to his manor; housed him, deluged him with the classics for his expanding education; surrounded him with lords and ladies of the court for his delight; lavished on him all the luxuries and privileges wealth could buy and an artful, sophisticated older man could imagine. Through this means, these gentlemen assert (without in the least bothering their scholarly heads about proof), Shakespeare came to write so intimately of the aristocrats, and of royalty.

A pleasant fairyland, this.

Examine the logic behind all these theories; the logic from which all belief in Shakespeare's authorship stems:

The major premise, always arrived at a priori, is that Shakespeare wrote the Works in the first place. Thus, this mode of reasoning begins where it should, in fact, end. How, under such a system of reasoning, can the authorship of the Works ever possibly be objectively weighed?

There are, of course, some less illogical scholars—who, while upholding the Shakespearean tradition, do not deny

9

the paucity of literary facts about their hero. William Allan Neilson sums up this school of belief:

> How Shakespeare learned to read and write his own tongue we do not know.

Dr. Neilson concludes, however, with a perfect example of sophistry:

> That he [i.e., Shakespeare] did learn needs hardly to be argued.

Perhaps not by you, Dr. Neilson. But certainly by me. This mode of rationalization is insupportable. Until proof is given of Shakespeare's education, or his means to such an education; until emotional conclusions are avoided, and logic substituted; until the name "Shakespeare" ceases to be the symbol of an emotional, almost a religious, faith, there can be no objective analysis. The problem of Shakespeare's authorship demands objectivity—and the application of reason.

2

ONE critic, Sir Edmund K. Chambers, in his work *William Shakespeare* has sufficient critical objectivity to tell us this about Shakespeare's education and literary reputation up to his thirtieth year:

> After all the careful scrutiny of clues and all the patient balancing of possibilities, the last word of a self-respecting scholarship can only be that of nescience. [Nescience: the state of not knowing; ignorance, due either to the nature of the human mind or of external things.]

Why, then, does even the liberal fringe of Shakespearean scholarship admit Shakespeare's lack of sufficient preparation or knowledge which any writer must have in order to write at all, and in the same breath grant Shakespeare's claim to the Works he is supposed to have written?

Surely there is a blind spot here—for how can one square a life which admits neither of preparation nor of education with the creation of most complex and beautiful verse dramas ever written? I can only explain this as the idolization of the name "Shakespeare." The tearing apart of the basic fabric of logic is not explainable to me by any other means.

Incongruity is piled on incongruity.

The cause of this blindness is, as I have already said, idolization, and perhaps an unconscious faith, molded by four hundred years of a belief that Shakespeare did write his Works.

Scholarship deified the name of an author just as it idolized the holy products of his mind. But we are driven at this juncture to demand (apart from faith) why students, and generations of learned men, the "Shakespeare lovers," have accepted the man Shakespeare as the undoubted author of the plays and poems. Inspiration, as we have seen, could not have provided the genuine author with the classical and general knowledge necessary to write what he did. In the same way, faith could not, at the beginning, have generated belief in Shakespeare's authorship. There must have been a reason to begin with.

How did the Stratford son of a tradesman, the London actor of later years, become *identified* with the plays and poems that bear his name?

Let me continue my argument by recording, in chronological order, what we know of the datable and biographic facts of William Shakespeare's life from 1593 to 1598:

1594.... He is for the first time listed as an actor in the Lord Chamberlain's Company of Players.

1596.... William Wayte craves sureties of the peace against William Shakespeare and others.

1596-1598.... He is assessed for taxes as a resident of St. Helen's Parish, Bishopsgate, London.

1597.... He purchases "New Place," a house in Stratford.

1598.... He is interested in purchases of land in Shottery.

1598.... His name is entered among the chief holders of corn and malt at Stratford.

1598.... He lends one Richard Quyny thirty pounds.

1598.... He is listed as an actor in the cast of Ben Jonson's *Every Man in His Humour.* This was not mentioned, however, until 1616.

These eight facts are all that is known of the author of *Macbeth, Timon of Athens,* and *Hamlet,* between his thirtieth and thirty-sixth years. Not a record exists of a personal reference, verbal or written, from others about him, to others from him, as a practicing writer. The two literary commentaries (1594 and 1598) refer to the already published poems, *Venus and Adonis* (1593) and *The Rape of Lucrece* (1594), which merely bore the name "William Shakespeare" in the secondary pages of the books.

Only twice then, to recapitulate, is Shakespeare's name imprinted in the secondary pages of books. These are the only two times he is observed at all in contemporary literature, between 1593 to 1598.

The question remains: How did William Shakespeare's name become associated with the Works?

Let me repeat that *Venus and Adonis* was the first published work that appeared with the name "William Shakespeare" attached to it, four months after—after—Christopher Marlowe's murder. The date 1593 is a critical one indeed in the Marlowe-Shakespeare relationship.

Shakespeare's name was not, mind you, affixed to the title page of *Venus and Adonis*; there was no by-line to signify his authorship. His name was written on another page, attached to an unauthorized dedication to Henry Wriothesley, the Earl of Southampton, who was 20 years old at the time—ten years younger than Shakespeare. In the dedication of *Venus and Adonis* the author explicitly states that the poem is "the first heir of my invention," in other words, the author's first work. The year is 1593. On another page-front of the book, two Latin lines from the 15th Elegy of Ovid's *Amores* are printed:

> Villa miretur vulgus, mihi flavus Apollo
> Pocula Castalia plena ministret aqua.

An interesting thing about Marlowe is that Ovid, in Marlowe's younger days, had been his favorite author-poet. Ovid became Shakespeare's favorite poet-author hard upon the writing that followed *The Rape of Lucrece*. Marlowe translated the entire book of Ovid's *Amores* while still a student at Cambridge University. The translation had been published as *All Ovid Elegies: 3 Books*. Marlowe translated the two lines with which Shakespeare prefaced his first work, as:

> Let base conceited wits admire vile things,
> Fair Phoebus lead me to the Muses springs.

Venus and Adonis (and this point must be stressed) was registered (not published) in the Stationers Company (the Elizabethan copyright bureau), April 18, 1593—six weeks before Marlowe's murder. There was no author's name attached to the registration. The poem was entered anonymously.

In September 1593, four months after Marlowe's murder, *Venus and Adonis* appeared suddenly in London, with the name "William Shakespeare" inscribed for the first time in a book. Never had the dramatist's name been connected in any fashion with any printed matter before this date.

Perhaps not so incidentally, many scholars and critics have commented upon the extraordinary resemblance of style and treatment between *Venus and Adonis* and Marlowe's *Hero and Leander*.

Interestingly enough, reputable Elizabethan students feel that both poems were written in 1593. This will be taken up at greater length later in my argument.

The first play that bears Shakespeare's name was *Love's Labour's Lost*, which was published in 1598—when Shakespeare was 36, when Marlowe was thought to have been dead five years. The play was printed as "newly corrected & augmented by W. Shakespeare."

Scholarship tells us that Shakespeare had written no less than twelve plays—possibly as many as sixteen—up to 1598. Until that year, William Shakespeare was not known either as a playwright or as a dramatist. It follows, according to this reasoning, that up to his thirty-sixth year (within four years of the average Elizabethan male life expectancy) William Shakespeare was unknown in any professional circle as a writer. Now, how could a man write twelve enormously capable plays, and possibly as many as sixteen, without causing one ripple of comment in the theatrical and literary world of his time?

Why is it, then, that the world believes Shakespeare wrote the plays that bear his name?

Because, and only because, the name "William Shakespeare" appears in the title page of some of the Quarto plays and in the posthumously published 1623 Folio edition of "Shakespeare's" Works. This is the basis for our belief that the London actor authored the Works that bear his name. A fragile foundation this, as I shall later prove.

But back to the period of 1598. Of the total 36 plays brought out in the First Folio of 1623, only sixteen were published in Quarto before that year. These were:

Titus Andronicus	published	1594
Richard II	"	1597
Richard III	"	1597
Romeo and Juliet	"	1597
Love's Labour's Lost	"	1598
Henry IV, Part I	"	1598
Merchant of Venice	"	1600
Henry V	"	1600
Much Ado About Nothing	"	1600
Henry IV, Part II	"	1600
A Midsummer Night's Dream	"	1600
Merry Wives of Windsor	"	1602
Hamlet	"	1603
King Lear	"	1608
Troilus and Cressida	"	1609
Othello	"	1622

The remaining twenty plays appeared in the First Folio for the first time. The 1623 Folio is the only source and authority for the twenty plays ascribed to Shakespeare. These twenty dramas, posthumously printed and made available for the first time in 1623, were:

> The Tempest
> The Two Gentlemen of Verona
> Measure for Measure
> The Comedy of Errors
> As You Like It
> The Taming of the Shrew
> All's Well That Ends Well
> Twelfth Night
> The Winter's Tale
> King John
> Henry VI, Part I
> Henry VI, Part II
> Henry VI, Part III
> Henry VIII
> Coriolanus
> Timon of Athens
> Julius Caesar
> Macbeth
> Antony and Cleopatra
> Cymbeline

The First Folio has been called the most precious volume of literature ever bequeathed the world. The volume is the sole authority for plays like *Macbeth, Antony and Cleopatra,* and *Julius Caesar.* Without the First Folio these masterpieces would have disappeared forever. Strangely enough, the bulk of these twenty dramas were never produced on the stage before 1623, so that the Folio's value is further enhanced.

Of the fifteen First Quarto plays published while Shakespeare was still alive—he died in 1616—only nine appeared with the name "William Shakespeare" attached to them. The remaining six First Quarto plays made their first appearance anonymously.

These are:

Love's Labour's Lost	published	1598
A Midsummer Night's Dream	"	1600
The Merchant of Venice	"	1600
Henry VI, Part II	"	1600
Much Ado About Nothing	"	1600
The Merry Wives of Windsor	"	1602
Hamlet	"	1603
King Lear	"	1608
Troilus and Cressida	"	1609

. . . And, therefore, a third phenomenon: of the thirty-six plays contained in the First Folio of 1623 only nine bore the name "William Shakespeare" in the First Quartos printed during the Stratford actor's lifetime. From the year Shakespeare emerged as a writer (1593) to the date of his death (1616), nine dramas, or 25 per cent of the total number written, were printed for the first time naming William Shakespeare as their author.

This is the only reason on which posterity bases its belief that Shakespeare wrote all the plays that bear his name, up to his death in 1616.

There is no other reason for so believing.

On the evidence of nine title-paged First Quartos, issued before 1616, out of a total of thirty-six dramas written up to that time, William Shakespeare has been immortalized.

Francis Meres, a divine and a schoolteacher, wrote his *Palladis Tamia,* a treatise on morals, religion, and literature; it was published in 1598. One section of the book compares English poets and dramatists to Greek and Latin writers of antiquity.

Almost every English poet of note who wrote up to 1598 is mentioned in these comparisons; more than twenty of them.

Included were Robert Greene, John Lyly, Thomas Heywood, Edmund Spenser, Thomas Kyd, George Chapman, Ben Jonson, George Peele, Philip Sidney, Thomas Nash,

Walter Raleigh, Anthony Munday, Christopher Marlowe, and of course William Shakespeare.

Meres mentions Shakespeare more often than the others, and specifically names twelve of his plays and some of his poems as comparable to the works of Seneca, Plautus, Horace, Homer, Sophocles, etc. Now the extent of Meres's reference to William Shakespeare and the other English writers is limited to critical judgment of their already published, staged, or at least circulated pieces. He avoids any allusion to Shakespeare personally or professionally. All he does is to reinforce the "title page evidence" and the general belief that William Shakespeare was the author of some plays and poems.

Sir Sidney Lee speaks of Meres's criticism as one of the "many testimonies paid to Shakespeare's literary reputation at this period of his career." There were in fact only two other "testimonials," an anonymous one prefixed in verse to *Willobie His Avisa* in 1594, and Richard Barnfield's verse-praise in *Divers Humours,* published in 1598. Neither personally identified Shakespeare as a writer.

But there is no reason to believe that Meres's allusions to Shakespeare constitute a proof that Shakespeare wrote the plays under his name. The average Elizabethan critic was in the same position by 1598 as most of our Shakespearean critics today—he had no reason to disbelieve Shakespeare's claims to authorship.

They all merely repeated the indicated authority of William Shakespeare. Christopher Marlowe's authorship was a unique, close-held secret. In point of fact, it was easier to keep the deception alive at that time than it might be today. The Elizabethan era was peculiarly susceptible to deceits and frauds. J. M. Robertson, Shakespearean student and authority, sums up this point of view about *Palladis Tamia*:

"As for Meres, he simply stated the claim of the theatre company."

It is not wise to read into Meres's 1598 allusion more than is necessary.

All of which leads us to an important point. Not only up to 1598 was Shakespeare never referred to as a writer, but during his entire life not one of his contemporaries ever identified him as such. Any reference to Shakespeare revolved around what he had already written, around those plays and poems to which his name was tagged. Before publication of Meres's *Palladis Tamia* in 1598, the following four plays had been anonymously printed:

Titus Andronicus	published 1594	
Richard II	"	1597
Richard III	"	1597
Romeo and Juliet	"	1597

These Quarto dramas appeared without the name of any author. Only three plays out of the roster of thirty-six ever carried Shakespeare's name in the register of the Stationers Company—up to 1623. Out of the total number included in the First Folio, three dramas were officially identified as Shakespeare's, in the Registry's records.

The Second Part of Henry IV	S.R. 1600
Much Ado About Nothing	S.R. 1600
King Lear	S.R. 1600

After Shakespeare's death, in 1616, at least fourteen Quarto plays, not acknowledged as his by most scholars, were published with his name imprinted in the title pages. We call attention to this fact only for the record. But it will bolster our thesis as we continue.

To recap our analysis of the authenticity of Shakespeare's authorship of his thirty-six plays up to his death in 1616: it has been seen that on the flimsy evidence of his name appearing in the title pages of the nine first Quartos the generalization that he is the author of the entire Canon has been made, and sustained, for far too long.

Here is my counterevidence:

During the prime of Shakespeare's years on earth—that is, between 1595 and 1611, between his thirty-second and his forty-eighth year, during the most prolific literary period of his life, there appeared in London eight published Quarto dramas title-paged and dated with the following inscriptions:

1595. *Locrine*..."Newly set forth, overseen and corrected by W. S." (Compare *Love's Labour's Lost,* 1598, title-paged: "Newly corrected and augmented by W. Shakespeare.")

1600. *Sir John Oldcastle*..."Written by William Shakespeare."

1602. *The True Chronicle History of Thomas Lord Cromwell*..."Written by W. S. Imprinted at London for William Jones and are to be sold at his house near Holborne Conduit." (Compare Christopher Marlowe's *Edward II,* 1594: "Imprinted at London for William Jones dwelling near Holborne Conduit.")

1605. *The London Prodigal*..."By William Shakespeare." Published by Nathaniel Butter (who registered *King Lear* with Stationers Company in 1607). *The London Prodigal* was registered in 1598 by Nicholas Linge, who also published *Hamlet* in 1604 and who registered Christopher Marlowe's *The Jew of Malta* in 1594.)

1607. *The Puritan*..."Written by W. S."

1608. *A Yorkshire Tragedy*..."Written by W. Shakespeare." This play was registered with Stationers Company the same year as "by William Shakespeare."

1609. *Pericles, Prince of Tyre*..."By William Shakespeare." Registered with Stationers Company May 20, 1608, by Edward Blount. (The same Edward Blount published Christopher Marlowe's poem *Hero and Leander* in 1598, and was one of the central figures in a syndicate of men who published the First Folio of 1623 by "William Shakespeare." We shall deal again with Blount later in the argument.

1611. *The Troublesome Reign of King John*..."Written by W. Sh." (Also published anonymously in 1591.)

Every Elizabethan student is familiar with these eight dramas. They know they were published concurrently with the printing of the canonical Quartos, during Shakespeare's lifetime.

Why have they not been acknowledged as Shakespeare's? If the case for his authorship is based on the testimony that the name "Shakespeare" appeared in the title pages of nine plays published during his lifetime, why are not these eight plays—which also bear his name or initials in their title pages, and which were similarly published during his lifetime —attributed to him?

Add to this the fact that some of these eight plays were printed and published by the men who brought out the nine Quartos readily acknowledged as Shakespeare's, and you have a mountain of incongruities. Why is one group of plays accepted as genuine and the other group rejected, when the criteria for determining the authorship of both are identical? Which group is genuine Shakespeare, and which not?

Let us assume that the rejected dramas are fraudulent; that unprincipled and unethical publishers printed them knowing that they were not written by Shakespeare. What evidence do we have, however, to confirm this assumption, and to deny, at the same time, the fact that these eight "rejected" plays were not written by Shakespeare?

What further proof or evidence, if you prefer the other side of the coin, has been offered to stamp the nine plays brought out by the publishers as definitely Shakespeare's?

The authority of title-page evidence is obviously untrustworthy. The objective reader will perceive that the yardstick by which Shakespeare's authorship is measured both accepts and rejects at the same time. Such a yardstick is valueless.

In the face of this display of inconsistencies the structure upon which Shakespeare's authorship rests up to 1623 topples. At best it is only a hypothesis and the truth remains to be proved.

What has been the status of these eight rejected dramas in the scholastic world during the centuries? They have been termed doubtful and of unknown origin, despite the fact that they were published en masse in the Third Shakespeare Folio of 1614, second issue, and in the Fourth Shakespeare Folio of 1685, both editions of which also included the 36 canonical plays, which, as you will remember, were published, by themselves, in the First Folio of 1623.

Why does *Pericles* alone rate inclusion in the Canon? Why does this play alone deserve acceptance when the other seven are still rejected? I shall return to *Pericles*.

Indeed, the present inclusion of *Pericles* in the canonical dramas may prove the Achilles' heel of Shakespearean scholarship.

As for the other documented facts of William Shakespeare's life, dating from 1598 to his death in 1616, none of them personally identifies him as a poet, a writer, or a dramatist.

Here are the remaining details of William Shakespeare's life, unencumbered by wishful thinking, legend, fancy, conjecture, and tradition, which have been gathered from sixty to ninety years after his death:

1599. He sells a load of stone to the Stratford Corporation.
1599. He becomes part owner of the Globe Theatre.
1601. His name is given passing mention in the will of Thomas Whittington.
1602. He is mentioned in an off-color story as the third party to an assignation.
1602. He buys a large tract of land in old Stratford.
1602. He receives assurance of title to his residence, "New Place," in Stratford.
1602. He buys a cottage and some land opposite New Place.
1603. He and his theatrical colleagues become the King's Servants.
1603. He is listed as an actor in the cast of Ben Jonson's play, *Sejanus*. (This was first mentioned, however, in 1616.)
1604. He is numbered among nine actors who receive a grant of red cloth for King James's coronation procession.

1604. He sues Philip Rogers, apothecary, for 35 shillings and 10 pence that he, William Shakespeare, supplied him.

1605. A bequest of 30 shillings is made to him in the will of Augustine Phillips, a fellow actor.

1605. Shakespeare purchases an interest in the corn, hay, and wool and lamb tithes of Stratford and other villages.

1608. He engages in a lawsuit against John Addenbroke of Stratford in which he sues Addenbroke for 6 pounds.

1609. Complaint of Shakespeare and other citizens to the Lord Chancellor regarding the tithes of Stratford.

1610. He increases his purchases of real estate from William and John Combes.

1612. William Shakespeare is mentioned as a witness in a dowry suit in the case of Belott versus Mountjoy.

1613. He purchases a house in Blackfriars, London.

1613. The mortgage deed on the Blackfriars property is filed.

1613. William Shakespeare and another actor receive payment from the Earl of Rutland for contributing to the devising of an impresa, or personal badge. (The authenticity of this document has been questioned.)

1614. A bequest is left to Shakespeare of 5 pounds in John Combes's will.

1614. From the diary of Thomas Greene: "My cousin Shakespeare coming to town [i.e., London]. I went to see him how he did."

1614. A legal agreement protecting Shakespeare against loss of tithe income at Welcombe.

1614-1615. Notes concerning his attitude toward proposed enclosures of property at Welcombe.

1615. William Shakespeare is involved in a lawsuit concerning some documents relating to his Blackfriars property.

1616. He makes his will, March 25, 1616. One month after, he dies. Three of his signatures are contained in the will.

1616. Shakespeare's death and burial recorded as occurring on April 23, 1616, in the Stratford Burial Register. He is interred in the chancel of Holy Trinity Church, Stratford, with an inscription carved in the monument showing date of his death.

The above details, added to those previously listed from 1564 to 1598, comprise the existing documented account of

Shakespeare's life. This, please note, is the author of *Antony and Cleopatra, Hamlet, King Lear*—a man who wrote his way into the heart of humanity with a pen of iron and gold. The fact that a man married; that he owed money, and was owed money; that he begat children and bought property— these are not of interest to posterity except as incidental, unimportant highlights. Certainly, they have nothing to do with the problem of determining authorship.

To sum up: from the date of his birth (1564) to the date of his death (1616) not a single piece of evidence (outside of his name appearing in the title pages of the nine First Quartos) has been found to attest that William Shakespeare was a writer or a poet.

There are, however, allusions by contemporaries to fourteen plays which were produced in London theaters during his lifetime.

These are:

> The Comedy of Errors
> Love's Labour's Lost
> Julius Caesar
> Henry IV
> Richard II
> Richard III
> Twelfth Night
> Hamlet
> Othello
> Macbeth
> Cymbeline
> The Winter's Tale
> Henry VIII
> The Tempest

Though these plays are mentioned, the author is not. The name "William Shakespeare" is never linked to any of the fourteen plays. References to the dramas consist only in the naming of their titles and mention of their plots and characters. There is no mention of Shakespeare.

The five remaining references contemporary with Shakespeare's life exist in connection with already-published or already-circulating manuscripts. These are manuscripts to which Shakespeare's name was tagged after 1593, after Christopher Marlowe's murder.

In this book and, indeed, in fact, William Shakespeare is on trial for his literary life. I believe that I have enough proof for conviction.

3

ON March 25, 1616, Shakespeare drew up a detailed will. I have examined a large number of Elizabethan wills, wills which were mostly those of aristocrats, who had large estates to dispose of. Not one that I have seen compares in length and detail to Shakespeare's. There are more than twenty people to whom Shakespeare makes bequests. His wife, his children, his in-laws, his grandchildren, and his friends—all are beneficiaries. He inventories his household goods and other material possessions; disposes of intimate articles such as a bowl, a sword, jewelry, and plates. He is specific enough to leave his wife his "second-best bed." His friends receive small sums of money with which to buy themselves rings in his memory. Cash and real estate holdings go, prudently enough, to his immediate family.

This is a practical, even an earthy, will, commonplace and conservative. It is also an indictment and a negation of Shakespeare's whole existence as playwright. There is no mention of plays or poetry. The will is the will of a man who obviously owned no books, since not one is mentioned. Had William Shakespeare owned even a few, they would surely have been referred to in his will, since books were valuable in Elizabethan times, and there is no doubt that the author of the Shakespeare Canon would have been required to possess at least a minimal number of books for his professional use—especially since all but two or three of the 36 dramas known as Shakespeare's are based on source books, domestic or foreign, in print at the time.

An examination of whatever documentary proof we have that Shakespeare existed would tend to prove that, whatever the man was, he was not a writer. It took me almost nineteen years to echo the words of Henry James: "I am haunted by the conviction that the divine William is the biggest and the most successful fraud ever practiced on a patient world."

William Shakespeare died in 1616 at the age of 52. For Elizabethan times, he lived to a ripe old age. Certainly he was older by far at his death than most of his literary contemporaries. George Peele died at the age of 39, Edmund Spenser at 47, Thomas Kyd at 36, Robert Greene at 34, John Fletcher at 46, Sir Philip Sidney at 32, John Webster at 45, Francis Beaumont at 32, and John Ford at 45.

As mentioned before, Shakespeare's literary output exceeded by far the preserved works of any other dramatist of his time. When writers of lesser stature and smaller renown passed on, their memory often called forth eulogies couched in verse form. When Shakespeare died in 1616 no public or private mention was made of him—as a man, a poet, or a dramatist. Among all the poets, dramatists, actors, friends, publishers, most of whom Shakespeare must have known, some casually, some intimately, not one was stirred enough to write a single elegy, a single phrase even, in memory of William Shakespeare. This is a situation that might conceivably exist in modern times, but Elizabethan convention demanded the elegiac poem as a mark of respect. Psychologically it is improbable that a writer of Shakespeare's stature would have departed life without mention from those around him. Even a shepherd, or a goldsmith famous in his trade, would have engendered some passing interest or mention upon his death.

Only Shakespeare's son-in-law, John Hall, a Stratford doctor, mentioned Shakespeare's passing in his diary: "My father-in-law died on Thursday." This, as far as I have been able to discover in the past three hundred years, is the only written reference to Shakespeare's death. J. W. Mackail, orthodox Shakespearean scholar, has said: "It is not a little remarkable that, in that copiously elegiac age, there is no trace of the decease of the greatest English dramatist and the foremost figure in English literature, having called forth at the time a single line of elegy."

But not until seven years after his death, in 1623, when the First Folio was published was Shakespeare given his due. From 1616 to 1623 not a single remembrance was made about William Shakespeare. Any objective scholar, no matter how orthodox his view, cannot help asking "Why?" Why was Shakespeare not remembered at his death nor for seven years after his death? Why did his friends and his literary acquaintances remain silent for seven long years? I submit that the formal tag "William Shakespeare" was a trade name of the time. I submit that the reason why Shakespeare was not eulogized was that his friends did not know him as an author or an artist of any sort.

The first formal Shakespearean biography was not undertaken until almost a century after his burial at Stratford. It took nearly a hundred years for enough interest to develop in William Shakespeare to call forth the sketchy *Life* by Nicholas Rowe. Rowe's *Life* was included in a preface to his edition of the Works published in 1709. It was, indeed, a sketchy and slipshod piece of research. Rowe relied for his profile of Shakespeare mostly on the legends and traditions that had begun to grow about him, obtained from men like Thomas Betterton, an actor, John Aubrey, William Beetson, another actor, Thomas Fuller, and William Oldys, and a number of not too reliable gossips.

Rowe admits that Betterton in 1708 made a journey into Warwickshire to gather up what remains he could of a name for which he had so great a veneration.

These men then pooled their gnarled remnants of information, which Rowe later collected and used in his book, at least fifty to ninety years after Shakespeare's death. And even the sources from which this information had originally been gathered were thoroughly unsubstantial. The material that Rowe put into his biography was composed of fiction, gossip, and sheer invention. Most of it discredited Shakespeare instead of honoring him.

To top it all off, most of these fanciful tales were invented decades after Shakespeare had died and, naturally, could not be corroborated. Rowe's *Life* cannot, therefore, be considered a definitive biography. Rowe had little factual material to go on. We cannot condemn him too much for swallowing every story, no matter how unreal, but strangely enough, Shakespearean biographers since Rowe have used Rowe's uncorroborated detail as their basic source material for their lives of the Stratford actor. Present-day scholarship, in point of fact, possesses more documentary knowledge of Shakespeare's life than Nicholas Rowe ever had at his disposal, since many of the facts were discovered only within the past two hundred years. J. W. Mackail confesses: "The most modern portrait of Shakespeare produced remains . . . largely (one) of inference and conjecture."

The facts, by their very meagerness, speak loudly. Nothing outside of title-page evidence identifies William Shakespeare as a poet or a man of letters. His life is rich in stories, embroideries; poor indeed in documentary evidence. Certain questions could well be asked of Shakespeare's first biographers were they alive today to answer them: Why did they not consult with Shakespeare's daughter, Susanna Hall, who lived at Stratford until 1649? Or his other daughter, Judith Quiney, who lived there until 1662? Or his granddaughter, Elizabeth Hall Nash, widowed in Stratford, who remarried John Bernard, and lived out her remaining years at Abington in Northamptonshire until 1670? Why did not these first biographers confer with the members of Shakespeare's own family who were alive when information was being sought about him as a man and a writer? It is possible that some of them were sought out but could give no information about their father as poet or dramatist, since they did not know him as one.

We are right back to the only palpable proof of Shakespeare's authorship: title-page evidence of nine First Quarto plays. Shakespeare's name, however, while alive, was printed in title pages of eight published plays rejected by conservative scholars. Thus these gentlemen cut the ground from under their own feet, since there is no more reason to believe that Shakespeare wrote the accepted plays than there is to believe that the nonaccepted plays are not his.

A curious paradox. The fact that Shakespeare had no possible opportunity to garner the education necessary to his later creative work; the fact that his last will and testament contains no reference to him as author or playwright; the fact that none of his friends or acquaintances mourned his passing as the literary convention of the times decreed they should—all this must be taken into account before unhesitatingly proclaiming William Shakespeare as the author of the Works that bear his name.

If not Shakespeare, then who? The poems and plays were written by someone. It is my belief, backed up by nineteen years of research, that only Christopher Marlowe, whose marvelous and tragic life we shall shortly begin to investigate, could have written them. But before submitting my case for Marlowe, let us investigate a statement that has brought forth much argument among scholars for nearly two hundred years. I refer to Robert Greene's *Groatsworth of Wit Bought with a Million of Repentance*. This little book has created more comment than any other single item in Shakespeareana. But first some background on Greene's pamphlet, written in 1592 and published the same year by a Henry Chettle, a friend of Greene's. Addressing his former play-writing friends, Greene cautions them against men of the theater. Specifically he roars against the actors, producing in his anger one of the severest condemnations against the art of acting in general, and actors in particular, that has ever been written. Greene accuses actors of cheating him of payment in the plays he wrote for them. They are, he fumes, apes, puppets, monsters, peasants, and parasites, living upon the life-blood of more creative men. He begins, pathetically enough, by imploring his playwright friends:

> If woeful experience may move you, gentlemen, to beware [i.e., of actors and men of the theater] or unheard of wretchedness entreat you to take heed, I doubt not but you will look back with sorrow on your time past and endeavour with repentance to spend that which is to come.

He then addresses, without naming him, one whom we all accept as the poet-dramatist Christopher Marlowe:

> Wonder not, for with thee will I first begin, thou famous gracer of tragedians, that Greene who hath said with thee like the fool in his heart there is no God, should now give glory unto His greatness. . . . Why should thy [i.e., Marlowe's] excellent wit, His gift, be so blinded that thou shouldst give no glory to the Giver? Is it pestilent Machivilian policy thou hast studied? . . . The brother of this diabolical atheism is dead. . . . Defer not with me till this last point of extremity.

Then, with what turns out to be prophecy indeed, he foretells Marlowe's future:

"For little knowest thou how in the end thou shalt be visited."

We now arrive at the paragraph that has caused such confusion and conjecture among Elizabethan students:

> Base minded men all three of you if by my misery you be not warned; for unto none of you, like me, sought these Burres to cleave; those Puppets, I mean, that speak from our mouths

31

those Anticks garnished in our colours. Is it not strange that I, to whom they [i.e., the actors] all have been beholden; is it not strange that you [i.e., the playwrights] to whom they all have been beholden, shall, were you in that case I am now, be at once of them [i.e., the actors] forsaken? Yes, trust them not; for there is an upstart Crow, beautified with our Feathers, that, with his Tigers heart wrapped in a Players hide, supposes he is as well able to bombast out a blank verse as the best of you; and being an absolute Johannes Factotum [i.e., Jack-of-all-Trades] is in his own conceit the only Shake-scene in a country. O that I might entreat you rare wits to be employed in more profitable courses and let those Apes imitate your past excellence and never more acquaint them with your admired inventions [i.e., plays]. . . . For it is pity men of such rare virtue should be subject to the pleasure of such rude grooms.

After some more literate cursing, during which he calls actors "peasants," "Painted Monsters," and "rogues," Greene concludes by warning his fellow playwrights against his wretched fate:

Delight not, as I have done, in irreligious oaths, for from the blasphemers house a curse shall not depart. Despise drunkenness, which wasteth the wit and makes all men equal unto beasts. Fly lust, as the deathsman of the soul, and defile not the temple of the Holy Ghost.

Abhor those Epicures whose loose life hath made religion loathsome to your ears. . . . Remember Robert Greene, whom they [i.e., the actors] have so often flattered, perishes now for want of comfort.

Whether or not the "actors" were responsible, Greene died shortly after the writing of this diatribe.

One hundred fifty years after Shakespeare's death, in 1766, Thomas Tyrwhitt, editor and scholar, came across Greene's *Groatsworth of Wit,* originally published in 1592. In reading the passage containing the synthetic noun "shake-scene," he believed that he had discovered a punning reference to Shakespeare. Here, therefore, was one allusion that partially bridged the exasperating nine-year silence in Shakespeare's life: those nine mysterious years between February of 1585, when he was already the father of three children, and the autumn of 1593, when *Venus and Adonis* appeared as "the first heir of my invention." The more Tyrwhitt indulged his wishful thinking the more he became convinced that "shake-scene" meant "Shakespeare."

He communicated his belief to his colleagues: men like Samuel Johnson, Edward Capell, George Steevens, Richard Farmer, and Edmund Malone. Improbable as this discovery seemed, these scholars, always eager for any literary straw that could be utilized in bridging the nine lost years in Shakespeare's life, immediately concurred with Tyrwhitt. From that time on, every Shakespearean scholar and researcher took Tyrwhitt's hopeful guess as gospel. Since 1766 this paragraph, or a facsimile of it, has appeared in almost every Shakespearean biography:

"In 1592 we at last meet with a reference to Shakespeare by a fellow playwright, Robert Greene."

And then, of course, fancy ran riot. If a word like "shake-scene" could be so interpreted, there was no end to the evaluation that could be given to the entire passage. The first to try his hand at this "sea change" was Edmund Malone, who in the late eighteenth century pointed out that Greene's line, "Tigers heart wrapped in a Players hide" parodied a line from Part III of *Henry VI:* "O tiger's heart, wrapped in a woman's hide"; that "an upstart Crow, beautified with our Feathers" meant that Shakespeare was plagiarizing the work of Greene and his fellow dramatists.

Other scholars offered other interpretations: Shakespeare (for instance) collaborated with Greene, Peele, and Marlowe and was gradually eclipsing them all as dramatist—therefore, the envy and malice of Greene's polemic. Or, other scholars saw in Greene's paragraph proof that he disliked a mere actor who aspired to surpass the writing of experienced playwrights—such as Greene. Still other scholars saw clear proof that Greene acknowledged Shakespeare as the author of the third part of *Henry VI*. And other interpretations, many other interpretations, one more ingenious than the next.

There was, of course, no unanimity in any of these fanciful phantasmagorias, except perhaps in one sense: most scholars agreed that the "upstart Crow," the "Tigers heart wrapped in a Players hide," and "the only Shake-scene in a country" were all references to William Shakespeare, the poet-dramatist.

To start, let us examine the words "shake-scene" and "Shakespeare." What, outside of a legitimate desire to account for the irritating nine years' silence, is the relationship between the two words? Greene was painfully, and unmistakably, referring not to a writer, but to an actor, in his paragraph—indeed, in his whole article. *Groatsworth* is a hymn of hate, not against playwrights, but against actors, all actors, and one particular thespian who had incurred Greene's special wrath.

Now, in his diatribe against this actor, he sought to use whatever ugly and angry epithets he could find. "Shake-scene" is an excellent one, only one of several, such as "up-start Crow," "peasant," "ape." Like its brothers, "shake-scene" was a term of abuse used in Elizabethan times against an actor who could bombastically "shake a stage with passion." In other and modern terms, Greene was calling this actor, simply, a ham. Ben Jonson, in his famous elegiac verse to the author of the First Folio, uses the term correctly:

> I would not seek
> For names; but call forth Thundering Aeschylus
> To life again, to hear thy buskin tread
> And shake a stage.

In *Othello,* Desdemona, speaking of her husband, observes:

> Some blood passion shakes your very frame.

Lady Constance, in *King John:*

> Then with a passion would I shake the world.

34

And the King, in Part III of *Henry VI*, comments:

What scene of death hath Roscius now to act.

Roscius, Roman actor, celebrated for his rolling stentorian voice, would have been a "shake-scene" of rare magnitude.

The author of the First Folio used the word "shake" more than a hundred times in various of his plays. The word was joined, for the most part, to emotional questions or sentences such as: "Is this the nature whom passion would not shake?" The word "shake" in *Groatsworth of Wit* was used as prefix to "scene."

We have today various brothers to this expression. We have in our theater "scene-shakers," "stage-shakers," yes, and even "shake-scenes."

Greene, I admit, capitalized the prefix "shake" when he wrote "Shake-scene." But he also capitalized more than fifteen other common nouns, of which "shake-scene" was merely one. "Puppets," "Antics," "Crow," "Players," "Tigers," "Apes," "Epicures," and so forth. The practice—the capitalization of common nouns—was not unusual in Elizabethan times.

Therefore, there is no reason to suppose that the common noun "shake-scene" refers to "Shakespeare," just because of the capitalization. And Tyrwhitt's great discovery becomes, like some other Shakespearean proofs, strained and perhaps a little absurd.

Who, then, was this actor—this "shake-scene"—whom Greene singled out for vituperation? There is no way of knowing; but I can allow myself a double guess: Edward Alleyn and James Burbage would both fit the definition to perfection.

Both men were famous actors. Both held interests in the flourishing theaters in 1592. Both would have engaged in business dealings with practicing playwrights, and either of them might have provoked Greene's anger.

This is, of course, only a conjecture.

Within months after *Groatsworth of Wit* appeared in print Henry Chettle published his *Kind Hearts Dream*. Chettle had brought out Greene's pamphlet. In the book Chettle apologizes to the playwrights whom Robert Greene had addressed, since the pamphlet had been "offensively by one or two of them taken."

Once again, scholars read into Chettle's apology a reference to William Shakespeare. Since they believe, for no good reason, that the actor "shake-scene" in Greene's pamphlet meant William Shakespeare—and since Chettle refers to playwrights he must have, they supposed, referred to William Shakespeare as one of the offended dramatists. And that reasoning is what lies behind the famous Chettle "reference to Shakespeare."

But, whoever the "shake-scene" was, he is unimportant to the matter at hand—Christopher Marlowe's authorship of the plays and poems known as William Shakespeare's.

Let us proceed to Marlowe.

4

IN the southeast corner of England lies the ancient city of Canterbury. It has been the ecclesiastical center of England and the seat of the Primate of the English Church since the seventh century. It is the Archbishop of Canterbury who crowns Great Britain's kings and queens.

Since Elizabethan times, Canterbury—with Canterbury Cathedral—has been England's spiritual oasis.

In Canterbury, on February 26, 1564, Christopher Marlowe, son of Catherine Marlowe and of John Marlowe, shoemaker, was christened. Two months later, in Stratford on Avon, in the County of Warwickshire, about 150 miles away, William Shakespeare was baptized—April 26, 1564.

Christopher was the oldest of five children. He had four sisters—Margaret, Joan, Ann, and Dorothy. A cobbler's living could hardly have yielded more than a basic livelihood for seven persons.

Christopher, however, must have been unusually intelligent. Before reaching his fifteenth birthday he was awarded a scholarship in the King's School, in Canterbury, one of the oldest grammar schools in the kingdom, more ancient even than Oxford or Cambridge. The King's School was attached to Canterbury Cathedral, and was administered by the Church.

Marlowe's scholarship originated with the Archbishop of

Canterbury, Dr. Matthew Parker, who died in 1575. The scholarship provided for

> fifty poor boys both destitute of the help of friends and endowed with minds apt for learning who shall be called scholars of the grammar school and shall be sustained out of the funds of the Church.

Young Marlowe qualified, since he entered the King's School on January 14, 1579. One of the more specific requirements was that a candidate for the scholarship should be able to read and create Latin verse. Marlowe, obviously, must have been able to do this.

At 14, Marlowe was able to compose verse that was the forerunner of creative efforts which Swinburne, three hundred years later, was to admire; and to say of its author that he was "the first English poet, the father of English tragedy, and the creator of English blank verse."

Marlowe remained at King's School for not quite two years. It is a matter of record that during his stay, the student-body presented various theatrical productions of "Tragedies, Comedies" and "Interludes." From this, we may conclude, Marlowe's passionate interest in the theater had its first impetus.

He must have been a brilliant scholar. He was nominated by John Parker, son of the deceased Archbishop, for another scholarship—this time to Corpus Christi College, at Cambridge University. One of the requisites for attending the college was that the students from the King's School

> must at the time of their election be so entered into the skill of song as that they shall at the first sight solve and sing plain song and that they shall be of the best and aptest scholars, well instructed in their grammar, and if it may be, such as can make a verse.

In December 1580, when he was not quite 17, Marlowe entered Corpus Christi, one of the fourteen colleges that comprised Cambridge University. He matriculated late for Elizabethan times, since most students entered the university in their fourteenth or fifteenth year.

Corpus Christi, while not a theological school in the purest sense, was a seat of learning where the religious theme predominated. Upon graduation, students were expected to become divines, especially those who came from the King's School, an institution whose policies were influenced by the ecclesiasts of Canterbury Cathedral.

Marlowe studied, therefore, in a university rich in prestige and tradition. He mingled with the sons of some of England's most illustrious families. He was a poor boy in an intellectual paradise. With the arrogance of the underprivileged suddenly transported to the world of luxury and privilege, he must have wiped from his mind all remembrance of his mother's kitchen and his father's workbench; of the stinking pallet of straw on which he had lain, surrounded by his four sisters. The lip service that he had been forced to pay religion, and religion's demands, during his grammar school period must have continued; but it will shortly be seen that it was lip service only: that beneath it a curious and arrogant mentality constantly compared, probed, reached conclusions that would have been shocking in any time and were terribly dangerous in Elizabethan England. The formative years of Marlowe's life invite a speculation outside the scope of this factual work. But here were laid the seeds of Marlowe's greatness—and the seeds of his tragedy.

While Marlowe was gathering experience and learning at Cambridge, London theatrical companies performed both classic and English drama at the university. Students also put on productions, and their presentations were enormously popular. As a matter of fact, students were encouraged to take part in the plays, and a statute of 1560, discovered in the archives of one of the colleges, ordered the expulsion of any student refusing to take part in a play's performance.

We know from ancient record that, while at Corpus Christi, Marlowe read most of the Greek and Latin authors available to him. Aristotle and Ovid absorbed him. In the poems and plays that he eventually wrote Ovid's influence, with his pre-Alexandrian hedonism and sexuality, was a constantly recurring theme. Some of the books that Marlowe referred to still repose on the shelves of the Cambridge library. Here we can still read the source books for *Tamburlaine*, written by minor Latins such as Ortelius, Jovius, and other obscure poets and dramatists.

Here, too, was Holinshed's *Chronicles*, which Marlowe first used as a dramatic source—and which W. S. was also, strangely enough, to use after Marlowe's "murder"—taking from it the plot for his drama *Edward II*.

It is probable that even before Marlowe was awarded his B.A. he had written, in his nineteenth and twentieth years, most of the plays that bear his name. Critics concede that during his undergraduate days he translated Ovdi's *Amores* and Book One of Lucan's *Pharsalia* into English; wrote *Dido, Queen of Carthage* and *Tamburlaine*, and two other dramas.

In the spring of 1584, barely past his twentieth birthday, Marlowe received his Bachelor of Arts degree from Corpus Christi. He then applied for a grant to renew his scholarship so that he could work toward his Master's Degree, the highest academic award in Elizabethan England. His request was granted.

He remained at Corpus Christi. In his twenty-first year, and after, he continued in his moments of leisure to write plays. He matured quickly and became more self-assured than ever. Strutting through the grounds of the ancient college, Marlowe was a young man who achieved what he wanted to achieve and who knew where he was going.

In June 1587 Marlowe was scheduled to receive his Master's Degree, after having completed the three remaining years of study at the university; but something happened just at the time when the degree was to have been conferred, and the university heads flatly denied Marlowe the fruits of his labor.

Records show that Marlowe had taken unauthorized leave from the university a few months before completing his final year. Class attendance, then as now, was obligatory. Perhaps this unauthorized absence was the reason the university withheld his degree or, perhaps, Marlowe refused to take holy orders.

Whatever the reason, we do know that as soon as word arrived in London that the Cambridge authorities had barred Marlowe from his Master's Degree, the Privy Council dispatched a governmental order to the university officials. It was signed in the Queen's name, which made it a categorical imperative.

Evidently, Marlowe wanted his degree badly enough to go to London and there to consult with, and appeal to, powerful friends. The following note has been discovered in the minutes of the Privy Council. It addresses the university dignitaries:

> Whereas it was reported that Christopher Marlowe was determined to have gone beyond the seas to Rheims and there remain, their Lordships thought good to certify that he behaved himself orderly and discreetly whereby he had done her Majesty good service, and deserved to be rewarded for his faithful dealing. Their Lordships request that the rumour thereof should be allayed by all possible means and that he should be furthered in the degree he was to take this next Commencement; because it was not her Majesty's pleasure that anyone employed as he had been in matters touching the benefit of his country should be defamed by those ignorant in the affairs he went about.

Marlowe received his Master's Degree shortly thereafter.

But why did one of the most powerful groups of men in England intercede for Christopher Marlowe? The note stated that Marlowe was determined to have gone "beyond the seas to Rheims" and "there remain." Then comes the quick assurance that "their Lordships thought good to certify that he had no such intent."

Marlowe's times were politically dangerous. Elizabeth's throne was slippery, though gilded. Mary of Scotland was ambitious and alive, though powerless. The latter's Catholic friends in many countries were plotting to depose Protestant Elizabeth and to crown Mary as England's Catholic queen. Both ladies had equal right to the throne, and the rivalry was intense and bitter.

Catholic machinations had the connivance of the King of Spain, and the machinery of treason was being cast in France. Plot and counterplot built one upon the other, in a crazy quilt of intrigue and bribery. There were intricate English spy systems in Europe, spying upon Mary's friends and upon each other. Renegade Englishmen—faithful Catholics, most of them—were involved in plots against the crown and, when discovered, were disposed of effectively and brutally.

At the head of Elizabeth's vast, complex espionage and counterespionage system was Sir Francis Walsingham, Secretary of State, honorable member of the Privy Council. Walsingham boasted as many as seventy spies in his employ to track down traitors. It was all violent and sinister.

A favorite rendezvous for British Catholics was the Cathedral City of Rheims, where, as English Jesuits, they assembled at the seminary to instruct Roman Catholic pupils in the art of English revolution. Marlowe must have known of these events. He speaks of them in his play, *The Massacre of Paris.* One character says to another:

> Did he not draw a sort of English priests
> From Douai to the Seminary at Rheims,
> To hatch forth treason against their natural Queen?

No wonder their Lordships certified that Marlowe had no

intention of going beyond the seas to Rheims, there to remain. The implications were gruesome.

The likelihood is that Marlowe's absences from the university were due to his trips to Rheims. But he went there as a spy, not as a traitor. And his employer was Sir Francis Walsingham.

The scene can be imagined. Marlowe returns to the university after fulfilling his duties as spy for her Majesty in Rheims. News has leaked to the university officials that Marlowe has been seen in the French city; that he may well have turned Catholic and traitor. Shivering in their robes of authority, the university officials do the only thing they can; they refuse Marlowe his Master's Degree and toss uneasily in their beds at night, wondering if even this repudiation is enough to make them loyal in the eyes of the Queen.

Marlowe returns, to find that his efforts on behalf of his government have gone unrewarded. Off he goes to London, to My Lord Francis Walsingham, who listens to Marlowe and calls together the Privy Council—Marlowe receives his Master's Degree.

In 1589 Sir Francis' cousin, Thomas Walsingham, inherited Scadbury Park in Chislehurst, Kent, a village twelve miles southeast of London. His estate consisted of over a thousand acres, and the manor over which he was lord dated from the thirteenth century. It extended into many adjacent villages and towns. The house, surrounded by a moat, nestled in the heart of a forest, surrounded by orchards, glens, fruit trees— the retreat of an aristocratic gentleman.

Walsingham was rich. He married beautiful Audrey Shelton, who as she became Lady Walsingham became, too, Lady of the Bedchamber to the Queen. Sir Thomas was liked at court, and in 1597, when he was knighted, the Queen herself came to Scadbury Park to bestow his title upon him, and lingered for a few days in the moated main house. He thus had access to the most powerful human being in the realm.

Walsingham was interested in the arts. He was known as a patron of poets, intimate with such writers as Thomas Watson, who in turn knew Marlowe well. Perhaps it was through Watson's offices that Marlowe and Walsingham met.

The relationship between the two men was of a sort only too common in Elizabethan times. It will become apparent that Marlowe became Walsingham's friend and lover. Marlowe must undoubtedly have felt himself safe enough from all political and religious danger to act as he wished. Because of this tie with Walsingham, which was unnaturally strong, the imposture upon which my argument is based is made possible. As for the exact date the Marlowe-Walsingham intimacy first began, no one knows. But there is reason to believe that it existed while Marlowe was a student at Cambridge. It continued inviolate for at least a quarter of a century—even perhaps until a few years before the publication of the First Folio, in 1623.

Keeping Sir Thomas Walsingham as an ever-present background figure, let us follow Christopher to London. At 23 in 1587, with his coveted Master's Degree, he proceeded to the cultural and social center of his world carrying a bundle of manuscripts that were to take theatrical London by storm. *Tamburlaine* was produced before he even arrived, and the Lord Admiral's Company quickly presented the newly delivered plays. Marlowe was suddenly and unmistakably a hit. His success inflamed his fellow dramatists, among them Robert Greene, who railed against Marlowe and against Marlowe's plays as early as 1588.

There is some likelihood that during his years in London Marlowe found himself occasionally employed as an actor. Many suggestions that have reached us through the centuries make this probable. The earliest of them date from 1675. But it was John Payne Collier who, in 1836, first called attention to the fact that he had in his possession an authentic though anonymous, Elizabethan manuscript—a ballad called

"The Atheist's Tragedy," in which the adventures of a character named Wormall, an obvious anagram for Marlowe, are depicted. There are many stanzas to the doggerel, but our attention is directed to the fifth and sixth.

> A poet was he of repute
> And wrote full many a play
> Now strutting in a silken suit
> Then begging by the way.
>
> He had also a player been
> Upon the Curtain stage
> But broke his leg in one lewd scene
> When in his early age.

Though Collier was a student of Elizabethan literature, and a good one, he had earned an odorous reputation among critics as a forger. Any documents referring to Shakespeare and his era produced by Collier were immediately held suspect. Scholarship promptly rejected "The Atheist's Tragedy" as not authentic.

Was it a forgery? I do not know.

But it is significant, in the light of my thesis that Marlowe lived on to write the works we know as William Shakespeare's, that the ballad speaks of an "atheist"—when atheism was the charge for which Christopher Marlowe was eventually arrested and which led to the necessity of his "assassination."

According to Collier's ballad, Wormall was an atheist who

> . . . had also a player been
> Upon the Curtain stage
> But broke his leg in one lewd scene
> When in his early age.

It is significant because in Sonnet 37 William Shakespeare speaks of his physical affliction:

> As a decrepit father takes delight to see
> His active child do deeds of youth,
> So I, made lame by fortune's dearest spite

45

Take all my comfort of thy worth and truth;

> So that I am not lame, poor, nor despised.

and again in Sonnet 89, William Shakespeare refers to his affliction:

> Say that thou didst forsake me for some fault
> And I will comment upon that offense:
> Speak of my lameness, and I straight will halt
> Against thy reasons making no defense.

Is it coincidence that the character in the ballad, "Wormall" —or Marlowe, if you will—broke his leg? And that Sonnets 37 and 89 of Shakespeare speak of the author's lameness? Is it coincidence that the ballad's hero was called an atheist, and that Marlowe also enjoyed a reputation as the most outspoken atheist of his time?

Again, what could Collier hope to gain by forging this ballad? And how could he have so accurately invented a jingle whose protagonist was (a) a poet, (b) a playwright (c) an actor, (d) an atheist, and an atheist who "broke his leg"? How could Collier have imagined such detail? And why those particular details? Could he have hit upon these truths by chance?

I doubt it. Collier did not forge the ballad to carry out any argument that Marlowe wrote the Works of Shakespeare since he never gave a second's thought to such a possibility. There would seem to be no motivation. Perhaps he had none and the ballad is genuine, after all.

If the ballad is not a forgery, then it is one of the many links in a chain of evidence that points to Christopher Marlowe as the author of the works of the man known as William Shakespeare.

5

IN September 1589, at the age of 25, Marlowe was in London—and in trouble. He was involved in a duel which could have cost him his life, and indeed did cost the life of one of the participants. It seems that one William Bradley, age 26, son of a London innkeeper, had in the summer of that year craved "sureties of the peace against Hugo Swift, John Allen, and Thomas Watson." He was appealing, in point of fact, to the Court of the Queen's Bench for protection against the three men, who, he said, were threatening his life. It was the custom in Elizabethan England for any citizen, whose life stood in jeopardy because of verbal or written threats, to compel the offender to appear before the authorities and give security against such an assault taking place.

This is what William Bradley had done. The court ordered the petition against the three men returnable some three months later, during which time Bradley had unfortunately been slain by one of them.

We know that Thomas Watson, the poet—one of the three men cited in the above order—was a friend of Christopher Marlowe's. Being friends, we can deduce that the chances are that Bradley was not well disposed toward Marlowe either.

At any rate, on the 18th of September 1589, between two and three o'clock of the afternoon, in a street called Hog Lane, near the Liberty of Folgate, where Marlowe lived, and in the vicinity of the Theatre and the Curtain where his plays were performed, Bradley and Marlowe were engaged in a deadly duel. Records confirm the fact that both men's swords and daggers were brandished, with serious and deadly intent.

No one knows who began the fight. Perhaps Bradley resented Marlowe's intimacy with Watson and was venting his hate against a man close to the man he feared most. A delighted crowd of Elizabethan rubbernecks gathered around. Hearing the disturbance, Thomas Watson dashed to the scene of the duel, pushed his way through the crowd, and saw Marlowe defending himself against the attack of Bradley.

Watson drew his own sword in an effort to separate the fighters (at least, that was the story he told the coroner). Bradley, seeing Watson, left Marlowe and concentrated his attack on his real enemy.

"Art thou now come?" The coroner's report quotes Bradley as having asked the question and then answered it himself: "Then I will have a bout with thee."

Marlowe withdrew from the fight as both men went to't. Soon Watson slipped and suffered some bad stab wounds. Bleeding profusely, he retreated into a ditch. Bradley had him cornered. He set himself for the coup de grâce, when Watson, seeing an opening, ran his sword through Bradley's right breast to a depth of six inches and the width of one.

Bradley gasped, dropped, and died. Marlowe and Watson did not flee; and they were arrested for the murder. Both were committed to Newgate Prison to await the court's pleasure. The following day the coroner's inquest was held and, after examining Bradley's body and the circumstances of the fight, exonerated Christopher Marlowe of all responsibility, on the grounds that he had "withdrawn himself and ceased from fighting" before Bradley was murdered.

Twelve days later Marlowe regained his freedom after complying with some necessary legal formalities.

Thomas Watson was charged with Bradley's homicide. Fortunately the coroner's jury determined that Marlowe's friend had killed his opponent in "self-defense" and therefore neither feloniously nor with malice aforethought. Watson was remanded to Newgate, where he waited five long and dreary months before Queen Elizabeth (at the request of the court) signed the royal pardon, setting him free.

The circumstances of Marlowe's own "death" four years later were to prove suspiciously similar to the Bradley-Watson fracas.

It is intriguing, in the light of my belief that Marlowe lived on past his staged death to write the works of "Shakespeare," to read what one conservative commentator, John Bakeless, in his biography of Marlowe, concluded about the brawl just described:

> It was the exact situation of the duel between Tybalt and Mercutio with Romeo interposing. Shakespeare, who certainly knew Marlowe [there is not a jot of evidence to support this speculation], and who certainly heard all about this particular duel [again speculation], might easily have modelled the fight in "Romeo and Juliet" upon it. But Marlowe, wiser than Mercutio, dropped out of the fight as he saw his friend approaching, and Bradley turned his sword against Watson alone.

Could it not have been *Marlowe* who remembered this startling episode which he later so dexterously wove into *Romeo and Juliet*—a play which even some orthodox critics concede he must have had a hand in writing?

Presently I shall try to prove that Marlowe was not the man assassinated that fateful day in May 1593, and that he could have written *Romeo and Juliet,* and the other First Folio plays besides; that the name "Shakespeare" was attached to those plays by the hand of necessity only. It is certain that, if Marlowe did live to write *Romeo and Juliet,* he must have never forgotten that afternoon in Hog Lane when he saw his best friend wounded, and another man die, his face dabbled with the filth of the street in which he lay, and the rabble of London swarming over his body with clawing, thieving fingers.

49

𝔥

𝕿HE orthodox Marlowe Canon comprises seven plays, one
epic poem, two translations from the Latin, and many
lyric poems, the list of which follows:

Plays

Tamburlaine
Tamburlaine, Part II
Dr. Faustus
The Jew of Malta
King Edward II
The Tragedy of Dido
The Massacre of Paris

Translations

Ovid's Elegies
The First Book of Lucan's Pharsalia

Epic Poems

Hero and Leander

Lyric Poems

The Passionate Shepherd to His Love
Description of Seas, Waters and Rivers
Many Lesser Poems

Most scholars admit that Marlowe must be credited with
a far greater number of plays than those listed above and
that, as proved by the fingerprints of style, Marlowe must
be credited with at least ten other dramas—apocryphal or
falsely credited—not including, of course, the 36 plays, 2

poems, and 154 sonnets that appeared in 1623, probably after his death, under another name.

There is every right to assume that Marlowe was a prolific dramatist from the start. He began to write when he was a Cambridge University undergraduate at the age of 17, and he continued to work uninterruptedly until his arranged "assassination" at the age of 29.

Nearly thirteen years of writing, loosely figured, should have yielded a literary bonanza—especially from the fecund mind that was Marlowe's. Consequently, there remains a cluster of plays outside the Canon, and the dramas regarded as Shakespeare's, that should rightfully be laid to Marlowe's hand. Among these I include *Locrine, Edward III,* and *The Spanish Tragedy*—the last-named anonymously published but attributed to Thomas Kyd by Thomas Heywood twenty years after Marlowe's alleged murder.

Incidentally, it should be noted that Thomas Kyd and Christopher Marlowe wrote and worked together in the same London room in 1591. Kyd himself tell this to us.

Were *The Spanish Tragedy* once and for all attributed to Marlowe, Elizabethan scholarship would rid itself of one of its most vexing problems. The ancient puzzle of who wrote the "Ur Hamlet" would be solved. Under this hypothesis, the author of the 1604 Quarto *Hamlet* would have invoked his author's prerogative and called upon the source play of the same name, which source play, in turn, had *its* roots in *The Spanish Tragedy;* since all these play plots are identical.

But back to Christopher Marlowe. Renaissance London was a unique city. Its intellectual climate was much like its weather—stormy, foggy, lit with sudden brilliance; flashes of sunlight which illuminated such men as Thomas Harriot, mathematician and astronomer; Walter Warner, mathematician; Sir Walter Raleigh and his brother Carew; the Earl of Northumberland; and among all these, Christopher Marlowe walked and talked: the intimate of a clique whose thinking and observation was centuries ahead of its time. Arm in arm with barbarity, aficionados of the Code Duello, libertines and spendthrifts, these men still found time to think solidly, carefully, and with an admirable lack of fear. A wonderful company, indeed, for a young poet with fierce curiosity and a soaring mind.

All these men, brilliant as they were, were occupied in freeing themselves from the shackles of the medieval Church; an organization which still gripped tightly the timidities of men. Religion was based at that time upon fear, and the fear was considered holy. Not only did the Elizabethan fear God, but he feared, in the same manner, all thinking, reasoning, and social analysis which in any way disturbed the balance of power, and of class, that the Church had canonized.

It was unfortunate for the times, but the Elizabethan intellectual was almost inevitably a rationalist. The Church had penetrated into all fields of human endeavor. When faith and reason collided, faith usually won.

"Atheism," like "communism" in the Western world today, was on many occasions a word used maliciously. It was a word to fear. Atheism was a crime punishable by death.

This group, then, this collection of minds which sought to think dangerously, numbered Marlowe among them. With the little-boy ritualism of the Elizabethan, they even gave their number a group name: the "School of Night" was one of them; sometimes known as "Raleigh's Circle." School of Night is an interesting title. It exemplifies the guilt which even this avant-garde felt in regard to their inquiries and researches. It hints of the Black Mass, of that religious substratum which worshiped the Devil as straight-facedly as it worshiped God, hoping that whatever the outcome in the battle between good and evil its devotees would be on the winning side.

Possibly with some of this cunning-fearful spirit, Raleigh's Circle tested the truths of Scripture and tried to measure the spirit of God. They applied what they knew of scientific method to the rationale of theology, and theology was found wanting.

In those days the application of logic was tantamount to atheism. Merely to question Scripture or divine law was blasphemous, and blasphemy was punishable by public burning alive.

Despite the illustrious members of the School of Night, which comprised some of the most powerful and glamorous figures of the late sixteenth century, the clique was forced to meet secretly. Elizabeth's powerful courtier, Sir Walter Raleigh, was "scandalized with atheism" (in spite of the secrecy) and was even arrested and taken into custody in 1594 on the charge.

Many of these intellectual pioneers met a tragic end. Those who had no reputation to uphold them, nor apologists for their dangerous questionings, met death by fire. One of Marlowe's Corpus Christi schoolmates, Francis Kett, was doomed to burn as a heretic in Norwich early in 1589. The memory of his execution must have lingered in Marlowe's memory. There were rumors that Kett had persuaded Marlowe to atheism while they were at school together.

But somehow, with superb illogic, the circle over which Raleigh presided felt immune to governmental decree. It met regularly to discuss proscribed subjects. Its sense of security must have come from consciousness of the power it wielded in the most influential state quarters. It is otherwise impossible to account for its defiance of the edicts against free-thinking. The Circle was known despite its desire for secrecy. Its unorthodoxies were bruited about.

Puritanical burghers of London loathed its existence. One was prompted to speak of

Sir Walter Raleigh's school of atheism by the way and of the conjuror that is master thereof [probably Harriot] and of the diligence used to get young gentlemen to this school wherein

53

both Moses and our Saviour, the old and the new Testament, are jested at and the scholars taught, among other things, to spell God backward.

Marlowe was even accused of seeking to convert young men to atheism and in a still-existing commonplace book there is a passage attesting to this belief:

> Mr. Aldrich of Dover . . . said Fineaux . . . learned all Marlowe by heart and divers other books. Marlowe made him an atheist. This Fineaux was fain to make a speech upon "the fool hath said in his heart there is no God." . . . Marlowe wrote "Hero and Leander," was an atheist. . . . Marlowe was an excellent scholar and made excellent verses in Latin.

Some modern scholars are ready to wipe the taint of atheism from Marlowe. Frederick S. Boas is one of them. He insists that members of the Raleigh Circle were

> wont to prove all things—to test by stringent dialectic the most sacred conceptions. The "atheist lecture" read by Marlowe to Raleigh was thus probably a closely reasoned discussion in scholastic form of first principles.

Others maintain it was Unitarian doctrine that Marlowe espoused, that he questioned only Trinitarianism and the historical accuracy of Holy Writ, that he enjoyed theological argumentation and took delight in examining the growing conflict between science and religion. To the average Elizabethan mind, however, any discussion of the Church and God was atheism, indeed; foul and spotted.

Here, then, was an explosive situation, one which needed only a spark to start a holocaust. That spark was created by Christopher Marlowe's own arrogance. It is too easy in these days of neo-Freudian analysis to say that Marlowe had an inferiority complex, that he never quite forgot the pallet of straw and the cobbler's bench that were part of his heritage. In the class-conscious world of Elizabethan England, such a past was bound to create emotional conflict. At 28, Marlowe must have known his powers. He broadcast his intellectual opinions recklessly. He was guilty of youth's great fault—imprudence. This gross imprudence came close to costing him his life. He bent neither his head nor his heart to the virtue of humility.

Naturally enough, Marlowe's fellow dramatists resented his enormous vanity. In retaliation and perhaps out of envy for his tremendous talent, they resorted to taunts and sneers, and referred to him as "the cobbler," "the cobbler's son," or even "the Canterbury cobbler." Schoolboy ragging, smacking of the public school; but it must have cut Marlowe to the quick.

He first created enemies, then underestimated them. His conduct invited the charges that were to blast his life. Among the many specific accusations he faced, the nature of which will be investigated in detail, was the one of homosexuality. This charge appears to be true. It is important to investigate it at moderate length.

First, as to inversion itself. The Elizabethan world was a public-school world, and the avant-garde of which Marlowe was a part was neo-Greek in concept, and nourished at Alexandrian springs.

It was a world of cliques, and of strong friendships among men. It was, too, an amoral world, with its corrupt court and corrupt princes. It was a world of small, swarthy folks, who probably spoke with what we, today, might vaguely call a brogue. The age was bursting with vitality and Rabelaisian appetites. The women were fecund, the men sensual. There is good reason for the Anglo-Saxon speech which fortifies much of Shakespeare's dialogue. This was a world of robust talk and robust action.

These men were great womanizers. Some of them, however, turned to their own sex for virile outlet. Of effeminacy in the modern sense, with its concomitants of transvestitism and feminine behavior, there was little or none. These men were males at all times. While they could, and did, indulge in unsanctioned practices, they were soldiers, duelists, poets, normal lovers, and adventurers.

Richard Baines, a government informer, and Marlowe's playwright-friend, Thomas Kyd, mentioned Marlowe's peculiar interpretation of the relationship between Christ and St. John. In Marlowe's *Hero and Leander* there is between Neptune and Leander implied sexual inversion. In the first act of *Dido, Queen of Carthage,* there are overtones of erotic perversion, and the open homosexual love between the adoring King and his paramour, Gaveston, in Marlowe's *Edward II* is apparent.

When Marlowe idealizes the love of males it is a tender and romantic love. A critic has remarked that the love between Marlowe's men is more fervent, and more passionate, than the love between his male and female characters. And, though none of this can be considered as evidence of personal involvement, one accusation made against Marlowe by Richard Baines would seem damning. In his charges, which were often foully blasphemous, Baines accused Marlowe of "loving boys." It is true that the group of men who made up the Raleigh Circle were known for "the diligence used to get young gentlemen to this school." This circle could, perhaps, have demanded more as an admittance fee than brilliancy and wit; and the possibility that they were all, from Sir Walter Raleigh on down, prone to sexual inversion must be considered.

It is significant that, up to his reported assassination in 1593, Marlowe is never identified with the opposite sex. It is possible that the records do not reveal a liaison which might well have existed. But from the details of Marlowe's life that we know today he was never linked to the opposite sex.

There is another odd fact. Sir Thomas Walsingham of Chislehurst was Marlowe's patron, as well as the patron of

Marlowe's poet-friend, Thomas Watson. Watson and Marlowe roomed together before the Bradley duel. We know from documentary evidence that Marlowe was living at Walsingham's home in Scadbury Park just eleven days before his alleged murder.

Most interesting of all—if my thesis that Marlowe wrote Shakespeare's works logically carries—is the affection with which the author of "Shakespeare's Sonnets" held an unknown male subject, the mysterious "onlie begetter of these ensuing sonnets, Mr. W. H.," which inscription title-paged the 1609 edition of the poems.

While Mr. W. H.'s identity has baffled scholars for centuries, it is a fact that he is addressed by the author in the most amorous terms. It is not sufficient to explain away this ambiguous expression as an Elizabethan custom of expressing one man's friendship for another in terms of love. The sonnets thrust deeper than this. They are emotional, romantic, often sensual. The dedicatee is one for whom the author feels, without question, a most passionate affection, in every sense of that term.

Who was Christopher Marlowe's secret lover, then—to whom these poems, written by Marlowe although tagged with Shakespeare's name, were addressed?

I believe this unknown lover to have been Sir Thomas Walsingham, Marlowe's lifelong friend and protector. And I shall attempt to further this belief as we progress.

Meanwhile Marlowe, both within the Raleigh Circle and without, continued to trumpet his dangerous opinions about. He bandied his convictions privately, in company, in sight of and in hearing of the general public. And the informers were there to note down every word and hurry away with them to the proper authorities.

Imprudence piled upon imprudence; and at last, Marlowe's immunity ran its course.

Even as early as 1588, when Marlowe was 24, he had not

escaped the charge of atheism. During that year Robert Greene, in his book *Perimedes the Blacksmith,* whining with his usual sourness about the failure of his own plays, ascribed his failures to his inability to

> make my verses jet upon the stage in tragical buskins, every work filling the mouth like a fa-burden of bow-bells, daring God out of heaven with that atheist Tamburlaine.

And again:

> . . . such mad and scoffing poets that have poetical spirits as bred of Merlin's race, if there be any in England, that set the end of scholarship in an English blank verse.

"Merlin" is an obvious pun on Marlowe's name, since he was known at Cambridge with the variant surname of "Marlin." As to "daring God out of heaven with that atheist Tamburlaine," the reference is unmistakable.

In September 1592 Greene wrote in *Groatsworth of Wit* of one who had said

> like the fool in his heart there is no God.

He further chastised Marlowe by asking:

> Why should thy excellent wit, His gift, be so blinded that thou shouldst give no glory to the Giver? Is it pestilent Machivilian policy thou hast studied? O punish folly! What are his rules but more confused mockeries, able to extirpate in small time the generation of mankind. . . . The brother of this diabolical atheism is dead.

In the early part of 1593—four or five months before Marlowe was to be mysteriously "slain," a government informer reported to his superiors:

> Marlowe is able to show more sound reasons for atheism than any divine in England is able to give to prove Divinity.

The report goes on to state that he persuaded "one Richard Cholmely to atheism." And from the words "Marlowe is able to show more sound reasons for atheism" he would seem to have rationalized religion rather than to deny God outright.

But he was taxing the patience of the authorities. While pressure had undoubtedly been put on them to let Marlowe alone, there was a limit to which protection could protect. Marlowe was ridiculing sacred belief. He could not be forever shielded from retaliation by the Church militant.

On May 11, 1593, the Privy Council dispatched the following warrant to the commissioners of the city of London:

> There have been of late divers lewd and mutinous libels set up within the city of London, among the which there is some set upon the wall of the Dutch Churchyard that doth exceed the rest in lewdness, and for the discovery of the author and publisher thereof her Majesty's pleasure is that some extraordinary paines and care be taken by you Commissioners appointed by the Lord Mayor for the examining such persons as may be in this case any way suspected.
>
> This shall therefore to require and authorize you to make search and apprehend every person so to be suspected, and for that purpose to enter into all houses and places where any such may be remaining. And, upon their apprehension, to make like search in any of the chambers, studies, chests . . . for the dis covery of the libellers.
>
> And after you shall have examined the persons, if you shall find them duly to be suspected and they shall refuse to confess the truth, you shall, by authority hereof, put them to the Torture in Bridewell [Prison] and by extremity thereof, to be used at such times and as often as you shall think fit, draw them to discover their knowledge concerning the said libells. We pray you herein to use your uttermost endeavour to the end the author of these seditious libells may be known, and they punished according to their deserts. And this shall be your sufficient warrant.

What had happened had been that Flemish Protestant refugees, having fled their country and crossed the Channel to escape Catholic persecution, settled with permission in London. In so doing they incurred the hostility of English businessmen, who complained of the strangers, saying that they

> contented not themselves with manufactures and warehouses but would keep shops and retail all manner of goods.

Opposition against the foreigners grew. Meetings were held to "incense the populace against them," for the purpose of ousting them from the country. This was mutiny—since the Queen's government had legally approved the Flemings' entry. There was uprising in the air, and the authorities acted promptly and resolutely. Rhymes and threatening placards began to appear. Here, in part, is one found in the Dutch Churchyard:

> You strangers that inhabit in this land,
> Note this same writing, do it understand;
> Conceive it well, for safe-guard of your lives,
> Your goods, your children and your dearest wives.

Police confiscated the threatening placard, and handed it over to the authorities. And there followed the Privy Council's order just quoted.

How was Christopher Marlowe involved in this political tempest?

The rhymed verse indicated, at least to the police, the hand of a professional writer. What more natural, then, for these simple folk to suspect a playwright and a poet? Several were suggested. One was Thomas Kyd. On May 12, 1593 (the following day), the constables searched his room and among his papers they found incriminating matter that surpassed by far that for which they were searching. This consisted of fragments of a theological argument considered heretical indeed.

Thomas Kyd was arrested.

The exhibit was duly titled:

> 12 May 1593
> vile heretical Conceits

> denying the deity of Jesus
> Christ our Saviour found
> amongst the papers of Thomas
> Kyd, prisoner.

There was an addition:

> which he affirmeth that he
> had from Marlowe.

Kyd, when he was arrested, knew what to expect. Perhaps it was this knowledge that led him to protest, with hysterical force, that the "disputation" found in his room was not his but Marlowe's. He surely cannot be blamed: the wheel, the rack, the hot pincers, and the water bag must have possessed his imagination. He was but a step away from torture. His efforts to implicate Marlowe were successful but they did him no good. He was dragged away to Bridewell, where he stayed until his pathetic release. He emerged broken in body and spirit and died in 1594, at the age of 36.

In prison, Kyd was "put to the torture," as the Privy Council had so soberly and meticulously ordered. Whether he was justified in charging Marlowe as the author of the dreadful theological argument, no one knows. But he was certainly punished a thousandfold for his cowardice.

In an undated letter written soon after the report of Marlowe's assassination, Kyd put on paper a document so personal and so revelatory that I quote most of it below:

To: the R. Honourable Sir John
    Puckering, Knight, Lord Keeper of
    the Great Seal of England
At my last being with your Lordship to entreat some speeches from you in my favour to my Lord, who (though I think he rest not doubtful of mine innocence) hath yet in his discreeter judgment feared to offend in his retaining me without your honours former privity, so it is now, Right Honourable, that the denial of that favour (to my thought reasonable) hath moved me to conjecture some suspicion that your Lordship holds me

in concerning Atheism, a deadly thing which I was undeserved charged withal, and therefore have I thought it requisite as well in duty to your Lordship and the laws, as also in the fear of God and freedom of my conscience, therein to satisfy the world and you.

The first and most (though insufficient) surmise that ever (as) therein might be raised of me, grew thus. When I was first suspected for that libell that concerned the state, amongst those waste and idle papers (which I cared not for) & which unasked I did deliver up, were found some fragments of a disputation touching that opinion, affirmed by Marlowe to be his, and shuffled with some of mine (unknown) to me by some occasion of our writing in one chamber two years since.

My first acquaintance with this Marlowe rose upon his bearing name to serve my Lordship; although his Lordship never knew his service, but in writing for his players, for never could my L. endure his name or sight, when he heard of his conditions, now would indeed the form of divine prayers used daily in his Lordships house, have quadred with such reprobates.

That I should love or be familiar friend with one so irreligious were very rare, when Tullie said "Digni sunt amicitia quibs in ipsis inest causa cur diligantur" which neither was in him, for person qualities or honesty, besides he was intemperate & of a cruel heart, the very contraries to which my greatest enemies will say of me.

It is not numbered amongst the best conditions of men to tax or upbraid the dead, "Quia mortui non mordent." But this much have I (with your Lordship's favour) dared in the greatest cause which is to clear myself of being thought an atheist which some will swear he was.

For more assurance that I was not of that vile opinion let it please your Lordship to enquire of such as he conversed withal, that is (as I am given to understand) with Harriot, Warner, Roydon and some stationers in Paul's Churchyard whom I in no sort can accuse nor will excuse by reason of his company; of whose consent if I had been, no question but I also should have been of their consort, for "ex minimo vestigio artifex agnoscit."

Of my religion and life I have already given some instance to the late commissioners & of my reverend meaning to the state, although perhaps my paines and undeserved tortures felt by some would have engendered more impatience when less by far hath driven so many "imo extra caulas" which it shall never do with me.

But whatsoever I have felt, Right Honourable, this is my request not for regard but in regard of my true innocence that it should please your Lds so to . . . s . . . the same & me, as I may still retain the favours of my Lord who I have served almost this iij years, how, in credit until now, & now am utterly undone without herein be somewhat done for my recovery, for I do know his Lordship holds your honours & the state in that due reverence as he would no way move the least suspicion of his loves and cares both towards his sacred Matie, your Lordships and the laws whereof when time shall serve I shall give greater instance which I have observed.

As for the libell laid unto my charge I am resolved with receiving of the sacrament to satisfy your Lordships & the world that I was neither agent nor consenting thereto. . . .

And thus (for fear me I grow tedious) assuring your good Lordship that if I knew any whom I could justly accuse of that damnable offence to the awful majesty of God or of that other mutinous sedition towards the state I would as willingly reveal them as I would request your Lordship better thoughts of me that never have offended you.

Your Lds most humble in all duties,
Th. Kyd.

In absolving himself of the charge of atheism, Kyd automatically accused Marlowe for the second time. At the time of his letter, however, he understood Marlowe to be dead and he, therefore, found himself free to indulge in every accusation he could muster.

How long Kyd remained in custody is unknown. Whether he was as innocent as he claimed is also a matter of question. One thing is certain. He paved the path that led to Christopher Marlowe's downfall.

Marlowe became a marked man. His hours of safety were numbered.

Six days after Kyd's arrest—on May 18, 1593—the Privy

Council struck. It ordered the arrest of Christopher Marlowe in a warrant issued to Henry Maunder,

> one of the messengers of her Majesty's Chamber, to repair to the house of Mr. T. Walsingham in Kent, or to any other place where he shall understand Christopher Marlowe to be remaining, and by virtue hereof bring him to the Court in his company, and in case of need, to require aid.

Walsingham's Chislehurst estate lay twelve miles outside London. It could be reached on horseback within a few hours. It can be assumed that Maunder took Marlowe into custody at his patron's house either the same day or the following day, May 18, or May 19, 1593, and that the poet-dramatist was lodged for a few nights in a London prison, there to await the pleasure of their Lordships. In support of these assumptions, here is an entry in the MS. Register of the Privy Council, dated May 20, 1593:

> This day Christopher Marlowe of London, Gentleman, being sent for by warrant from their Lordships, hath entered his appearance accordingly for his indemnity therein, and is commanded to give his daily attendance on their Lordships till he shall be licensed to the contrary.

Marlowe, once examined, was released on bail and ordered to report daily to "their Lordships" until a verdict on his actions had been reached.

The minutes of Marlowe's trial are lost to us. Certainly it must have been tense: visions of the stake must have been performing a danse macabre in Marlowe's head, as he remembered Francis Kett and the ghastly leaping flames.

Though Marlowe was arrested on serious charges, he was released on bail, as we have seen. He was no common criminal. There is no doubt that his powerful friends assured the proper people that he could be apprehended at will.

Now, 1593 was one of London's worse plague years. Thousands were dying of pestilence. Anyone who could leave the stricken city did so. I mention this because for centuries scholars have theorized that William Shakespeare "must have gone into the country" at this time to escape the plague. While there, it is assumed that he wrote *Venus and Adonis.* Scholars have also believed that Christopher Marlowe fled the city, and went to live at Walsingham's Scadbury estate, where he wrote the poem *Hero and Leander.*

Both poems are regarded by students of Elizabethan literature to be strikingly related, even down to the very essence of their style.

And yet Marlowe was prevented, by the command of the Privy Council itself, from leaving the confines of the city.

He must have been afraid. Elizabethan London in the grip of the bubonic plague was a den of horror. The death carts roamed the narrow crooked streets. From the diamond-shaped windows, plague nurses (for those who were lucky enough to afford such) threw the sprawled and contorted bodies of their charges into the filth of the gutters below, while with iron implements the cartmen lifted the bodies to their vehicle, piled them one on top of another like cord-wood, and continued their grisly creaking way. And Marlowe was forced to stay in the middle of this living death, with the stench of sulphur in his nostrils and the shrouded corpse of England's greatest city about him. The theaters were shut down. The streets were deserted. The court gardens were still and dark; no longer lit with a thousand lascivious firefly lanterns, which aureoled the paths of the gallants, as they chased their ladies in the soft summer night. The smell of death and of fear was everywhere.

Thomas Walsingham must have known the seriousness of Marlowe's condition before Marlowe knew it himself. He was privy to the Privy Council; his cousin, Sir Francis Walsingham, had at one time been a member, and Thomas still maintained connections with the hierarchy of her Majesty's government. Somehow these two men, bound not only by friendship but by a romantic if abnormal tie, must have met and Walsingham, always the businessman, the conniver, must have revealed his fears to his lover.

Something had to be done, and done quickly.

Even while the two men must have been talking the situation over, Richard Baines's note against Marlowe (received by the Privy Council on May 29, 1593) was sent to her Majesty. The charges (as transcribed from Queen Elizabeth's own copy) run as follows (partly excised) :

> Copy of Marlowe's Blasphemies as sent to her Highness.

A Note

Containing the opinion of Christopher Marlowe concerning his damnable opinions and judgment of religion and scorn of God's word.

That the Indians and many Authors of antiquity have assuredly written of above 16 thousand years ago, whereas Adam is proved to have lived within 6 thousand years.

He affirmeth that Moses was but a Jugler and that one Harriot, being Sir Walter Raleigh's man, can do more than he.

That Moses made the Jews to travell 11 years in the wilderness, which journey might have been done in less than one year, ere they came to the promised land, to the intent that those who were privy to most of his subtleties might perish and so an everlasting superstition remain in the hearts of the people.

That the first beginning of Religion was only to keep men in awe.

That it was an easy matter for Moses, being brought up in all the arts of the Egyptians, to abuse the Jews, being a rude and gross people.

That Christ was the son of a carpenter and that, if the Jews among whom he was born did crucify him, they best knew him and whence he came.

That Christ deserved better to die than Barrabas, and that the Jews made a good choice, though Barrabas were both a thief and a murderer.

That if there be any God or good Religion then, it is the

66

Papists, because the service of God is performed with more ceremonies, as elevation of the mass, organs, singing men, shaven crowns, etc.

That all Protestants are hypocritical asses.

That if he were put to write a new religion, he would undertake both a more excellent and Admirable method.

That all they that love not Tobacco and Boys were fools.

That all the apostles were fishermen and base fellows, neither of wit nor worth, that Paul only had wit, but he was a timorous fellow in bidding men to be subject to magistrates against his conscience.

That he had as good a right to coin as the Queen of England, and that he was acquainted with one Poole, a prisoner in Newgate, who hath great skill in mixture of metals, and having learned some things from him, he meant, through help of a cunning stamp-maker, to coin French crowns, pistolets, and English shillings.

That if Christ would have instituted the Sacrament with more ceremonial reverence, it would have been had in more admiration.

That Richard Cholmeley hath confessed that he was persuaded by Marlowe's reasons to become an Atheist.

These things, with many other, shall by good and honest witness be approved to be his opinions and common speeches, and that this Marlowe doth not only hold them himself, but almost into every company he cometh he persuadeth men to Atheism, willing them not to be afraid of bugbears and hobgoblins and utterly scorning both God and His ministers, as I, Richard Baines, will justify and approve both by mine own oath and the testimony of many honest men, and almost all men with whom he hath conversed any time will testify the same, and as I think, all men in Christianity ought to endeavour that the mouth of so dangerous a member may be stopped.

He saith likewise that he hath quoted a number of contrarieties out of the Scriptures which he hath given to some great men who in convenient time shall be named. When these things shall be called in question, the witness shall be produced.

(signed) Richard Baines

67

The theological accusations were terrible, indeed, but Baines had charged Marlowe with having said that "he had as good a right to coin as the Queen of England." God and Christ were one thing, Elizabeth's purse another. This threat, plus the charge that Marlowe was traitorously fleeing to Scotland with Royden to join Catholic Queen Mary's cause and that he intended to remain there, practically put Marlowe's execution date on the royal calendar.

And while all this went on did Walsingham and Marlowe talk quietly, perhaps even hopefully, while Walsingham racked his brains?

A few days after Baines's deadly report, literary London is informed of the quick "death" (not murder) of that "foulmouthed atheist and playmaker" Christopher Marlowe. Marlowe had escaped, in the best way he could. He was dead, and nothing could touch him now.

To some, the news brought grief. But for the average informed Elizabethan Marlowe's death was good riddance to bad rubbish. Solid burghers did not like atheists, or coiners of money.

Those few who were interested, and curious, remained so. No one knew how Marlowe had died. Rumor had it that he had died of the plague. There were some who hated him enough to write verse, and quite passable verse at that, upon his demise. In a book published in September 1593, called *New Letter of Notable Contents*, there appeared a poem by Gabriel Harvey, "Gorgon or the Wonderful Year," which was composed soon after Marlowe's death:

Is it a dream? Or is the highest mind
That ever haunted Paul's or hunted wind
Bereft of that same sky-surmounting breath,
That breath that taught the tempany to swell!

He and the plague contended for the game;
The haughty man extolls his hideous thoughts,

And gloriously insults upon poor souls
That plague themselves: for faint hearts plague themselves.

The grand disease disdained his toad conceit
And smiling at his Tamburlaine contempt,
Sternly struck home the peremptory stroke.
He that nor feared God, nor dreaded devil,
Nor ought admired but his wondrous self.
Alas! But Babell pride must kiss the dust.

Now, Harvey was an illustrious cosmopolitan who detested Marlowe. Harvey's brother, Richard, was rector of St. Nicholas Church, Chislehurst, one mile from Walsingham's Scadbury Park home. For that matter, Walsingham worshiped at St. Nicholas. He and his family even had prayed in their "own" chapel (Scadbury Chapel) within the church itself.

In the summer of 1593—the plague year—Gabriel Harvey visited Chislehurst to spend time with his brother Richard. It is not too much to assume that the death of Marlowe was discussed—after all, the dramatist had been living only a mile away, with the Walsinghams. He had probably visited at least once the church where Richard Harvey preached. In fact, Thomas Nash, in referring to Richard Harvey, wrote that Marlowe with his inimitable acerbity, had said that Harvey was "an ass, good for nothing but to preach in the Iron Age." No wonder the Harveys disliked Marlowe.

If his death was discussed, it must have been with considerable glee.

The point of this matter is that it seems improbable that neither Gabriel Harvey nor Richard Harvey knew anything of Marlowe's death. The matter must have been deliberately and efficiently hushed up. And the brothers were fed the same pap as all of London—that Marlowe had died of the plague.

With Marlowe's death an established fact (as far as his contemporaries were concerned), his memory lingered on only with a few Puritanical ministers. One of these wolfish divines, Thomas Beard, wrote a book, published in 1597 and called *The Theatre of God's Judgements,* a diatribe against moral iniquity. In this book Beard appears to have been privy, for the first time since 1593, to a completely different version of Marlowe's death. He seemed to know that Marlowe had not died of the plague but of something else.

In 1597, four years after the "plague" had struck Marlowe down, another end is granted him in Beard's book. Marlowe's death is described in the following fashion:

> Not inferior to any of the former in Atheism and Impiety, and equal to all in manner of punishment, was one of our own nation, of fresh and late memory called Marlowe, by profession a scholar, brought up from his youth in the University of Cambridge, but by practice a playwright and a Poet of scurrility, who, by giving too large a swing to his own wit, and suffering his lust to have the full reins, fell (not without just desert) to that outrage and extremity, that he denied God and His son Christ, and not only in word blasphemed against the Trinity, but also (as it is credibly reported) wrote books against it, affirming our Saviour to be but a deceiver, and Moses to be but a conjurer and seducer of the people, and the Holy Bible to be but vain and idle stories and all religion but a device of policy.
>
> But see what a hook the Lord put in the nostrils of this barking dog. It so fell out, that in London streets as he purposed to stab one whom he sought a grudge unto with his dagger, the other party, perceiving so, avoided the stroke, that withal catching hold of his wrist, he stabbed his own dagger into his head, in such sort, that notwithstanding all the means of surgery that could be wrought, he shortly after died thereof. The manner of his death being so terrible (for he even cursed and blasphemed to his last gasp, and together with his breath an oath flew out of his mouth) that it was not only a manifest sign of God's judgement, but also an horrible and fearful terror to all that beheld him.
>
> But herein did the justice of God most notably appear, in that he compelled his own hand which had written those blasphemies to be the instrument to punish him, and that in his brain, which had devised the same. I would to God (and I pray

it from my heart) that all atheists in this realm, and in all the world beside, would, by the remembrance and consideration of this example, either forsake their horrible impiety, or that they might in like manner come to destruction: and so that abominable sin which so flourished among men of greatest name, might either be quite extinguished and rooted out, or at least smothered and kept under, that it durst not show its head any more in the world's eye.

How did the news leak out that Marlowe was murdered, that he did not die of the plague? Details are impossible to establish. But logical inferences can be drawn.

After the publication of Beard's book, interest in the dramatist soared. The tale of his assassination had drama. His death was still an accepted truth. Everyone knew beyond doubt that Marlowe had died. The only question that remained was how.

It remained for Francis Meres to give a lecherous turn to Marlowe's demise. In his *Wit's Treasury,* published in 1598, Meres paints the dramatist's murder in scarlet prose:

> As Iodelle, a French tragical poet, being an epicure and atheist, made a pitiful end; so our tragical poet Marlowe for his Epicurism and Atheism had a tragical death. You may read of this Marlowe more at large in "The Theatre of God's Judgements." . . . As the poet Lycophron was shot to death by a certain rival of his, so Christopher Marlowe was stabbed to death by a certain bawdy Serving-man, a rival in his lewd love.

The story of Marlowe's "lewd love" weathered the centuries, riding piggyback on every succeeding biography. Up to 1925, every biography of Marlowe described the place and cause of his "murder" as " in a tavern brawl" over "his lewd love."

There were other accounts of Marlowe's murder. But no one knew where he had been killed. The information was finally supplied by William Vaughan, who in 1600—seven years after Marlowe's assassination—detailed the following in his book, *Golden Grove*:

Not inferior to these was one Christopher Marlowe, by profession a playmaker, who, it is reported, about 7 years ago [i.e., 1593], wrote a book against the Trinity: but see the effects of God's justice; it so happened that at Deptford, a little village about three miles distant from London, as he meant to stab his poniard one named Ingram, that had invited him thither to a feast, and was then playing at tables he quickly perceiving it, so avoided the thrust that withal drawing out his dagger for his defense he stabbed this Marlowe into the eye, in such sort, that his brains coming out at the dagger's point, he shortly after died.

This was a more definite account than the ones that had gone before it. It was in Deptford, then, that Marlowe was slain. This clue, so sophisticatedly thrown away by Vaughan, was to prove fortuitous in the centuries to come. The true details of Marlowe's end were beginning to filter through.

We have already seen how Christopher Marlowe's reputation as a dramatist was established while he was still young. We know that his play *Tamburlaine* was produced in London before he left Corpus Christi. We know too that such men as Thomas Nash, in a preface to the first edition of Robert Greene's *Menaphon,* published in 1587, refers to Marlowe as

the alchemist of eloquence, who, mounted on the stage of arrogance, thinks to outbrave better pens with the swelling bombast of a bragging blank verse.

And even in such envious passages Marlowe is still given due credit, although unwillingly.

Then Robert Greene in his *Perimedes,* published in 1588, refers to Marlowe as one who could

make (his) verses jet upon the stage in tragical buskins

and couples Marlowe with

such mad and scoffing poets that have poetical spirits as bred of Merlin's race . . . that set the end of scholarism in an English blank verse.

72

And again Greene, in the second edition of *Menaphon* (brought out in 1589), tells of a love passage in one of Marlowe's plays, christening it a "Canterbury Tale" told "by a prophetical full-mouth, that as he were a Cobbler's eldest son, would by the last, tell where another shoe rings."

Greene, we have seen, was an embittered man, his pen dipped in the gall of his own spleen. He kept snarling at Marlowe in such essays as his *Farewell to Folly* (1591), where he says "a pedler would even bargain for the sheets of 'Tamburlaine' to wrap his sweet powders in those unsavoury papers."

No, Greene did not like Marlowe. Then, in September of 1592, when Greene was near death, he seems to reverse his attitude in *Groatsworth of Wit,* becoming as fulsome as he had been damning.

"Wonder not, for with thee I will first begin, thou famous gracer of tragedians"—and Greene continues into praise that is almost unbelievable. Of course, he is still Greene, and he must praise negatively. Still, a question like this—"Why should thy excellent wit, His gift, be so blinded that you should give no glory to the Giver?" is less a question than it is high praise. The question arises: Why should Marlowe be the recipient of all this fulsomeness, barbed as it might be? What about William Shakespeare (five plays, first ascribed to Shakespeare in 1623, had already been written)?

Again, after the report of Marlowe's death had become fact in 1593, Gabriel Harvey, in his poem "Gorgon," gives Marlowe his usual mixed due. But such phrases as already quoted —"the highest mind" and one whose "sky-surmounting breath . . . taught the tempany to swell"—abound even in this welter of dislike.

There were gentler tokens of remembrance. A month after Marlowe died, George Peele, a playwright, in the prologue to his *The Honours of the Garter,* wrote of "Marlowe, the Muses' darling." Thomas Nash changed heart in his *Christes*

Teares over Jerusalem, and called him, among other things, "poor deceased Kit Marlowe."

Edward Blount, one of the St. Paul's Churchyard stationers, publisher of Marlowe's *Hero and Leander* in 1598, and later publisher of the First Folio of Shakespeare's plays, referred to Marlowe as "our friend . . . the man that hath been dear unto us." Thomas Thorpe spoke of "that pure elemental wit, Christopher Marlowe."

Marlowe had friends, then. His reputation as a writer was established, memorialized.

William Shakespeare's, on the other hand, was not.

Nothing is known of Shakespeare, the writer, until Marlowe's death. We know not whether he attended school; whether he read books; whether he spoke to others, or about others, in his field; who spoke of him; who wrote of him; who praised him, envied him, loved him, or hated him.

Nor did Marlowe and Shakespeare ever meet. There is no proof, direct or indirect, that these two men were ever acquainted, much less friendly.

The conclusion is inescapable. We know nothing of William Shakespeare before his appearance as a writer in September 1593, because there is nothing to know. He was, until that year, nondescript; another of the four million people living in England at the time. His status must have been that of any other actor, artisan, or tradesman.

It has never been established that William Shakespeare was ever a writer.

The greatness of Marlowe's works was recognized, not only by his contemporaries but by critics in ensuing centuries. Some thought his *Edward II* was more effective, in parts, than Shakespeare's *Richard II* (the denouement of both dramas being, incidentally, identical). Other students believe that Marlowe's *Dr. Faustus,* with its apostrophe to Helen of Troy in the last scene of the play, contains some of the most beautiful imagery ever set to paper. It begins with the lines:

74

> Was this the face that launched a thousand ships?
> And burnt the topless towers of Ilium?

There is an awesome similarity between Helen, Faustus, Romeo, and Juliet.

Faustus to Helen:
> Here will I dwell, for heaven be in these lips,
> And none but thou shalt be my paramour.

Romeo to Juliet (written about 1595):
> . . . shall . . . death . . . keep
> Thee here in dark to be his paramour?
> . . . Here, here will I remain.

Faustus to Helen:
> Was this the face that launched a thousand ships?

From Shakespeare's *Troilus and Cressida*:
> . . . Why, she is a pearl
> Whose price hath launched above a thousand ships!

This was, by the way, the only time William Shakespeare ever used the word "launched."

It could of course, have been coincidence that both Marlowe and Shakespeare conceived Helen, and conceived her in almost identical imagery . . .

Yet, Marlowe was dead—killed in a tavern brawl, over a "lewd love." Or so the world believed.

7

IN 1820, James Broughton, a literary antiquary, brooding on Vaughan's statement of 1600 that Marlowe had been "stabbed to death" in "Deptford, a little village about three miles distant from London," sent a letter to the rector of St. Nicholas Parish Church at Deptford, inquiring whether there was any record of Marlowe's burial. It was the first time that any scholar had picked up Vaughan's musty clue. The results were astonishing. Broughton received the following reply:

> In the Register of Burials at the Church of St. Nicholas, Deptford, appears the following:
> 1st June, 1593, Christopher Marlowe, slain by Francis Archer.

The scholars' world was awake now, with a vengeance. But even the most thorough research failed to identify Francis Archer. No record indicated who he was, where he lived, what he did. He might as well have never existed.

No one knew, furthermore, in what part of the churchyard Marlowe was buried. His body had been thrown into an unknown and unmarked grave.

Then, in 1925, the mystery cleared.

Leslie Hotson, 105 years after Broughton's research, discovered a document hidden in the archives of the London Public Record Office—hidden away for 332 years—which revealed the strange circumstance of Marlowe's assassination.

What Hotson found was nothing less than the original Report of the Coroner's Inquest, together with a postscript of the murderer's pardon, signed by Queen Elizabeth.

This document, dated June 1, 1593, was titled "Inquisition to Chancery," and drawn up by "William Danby, Gent, Coroner to the Household of our Lady the Queen." The Privy Council possessed a transcript of the report, minus the supplemental paragraph of the murderer's pardon. Both were written in Latin. The following is a version of the original:

Inquisition indented taken at Deptford Strand in the aforesaid County of Kent, within the verge, on the 1st day of June, 1593, in the presence of William Danby, Gent, Coroner of the Household of our said Lady the Queen, upon view of the body of Christopher Marlowe, there lying dead and slain, upon oath of . . . [there are sixteen named witnesses] who say upon their oath that when a certain Ingram Frizer, late of London, and the aforesaid Christopher Marlowe and one Nicholas Skeres and Robert Poley, on the 30th day of May, at Deptford Strand, within the verge, about the tenth hour before noon of the same day, met together in a room in the house of a certain Eleanor Bull, widow, and there passed the time together and dined and after dinner were in quiet sort together there, and walked in the garden belonging to the said house until the 6th hour after noon of the same day and then returned from the said garden to the room aforesaid and there together and in company supped; and after supper the said Ingram and Christopher Marlowe were in speech and uttered one to the other divers malicious words for the reason that they could not be at one nor agree about the payment of the sum of pence, that is, le recknynge there; and the said Christopher Marlowe then lying upon a bed in the room where they supped, and moved with anger against the said Ingram Frizer, upon the words as aforesaid spoken between them; and the said Ingram Frizer then and there sitting in the room aforesaid, with his back toward the bed where the said Christopher Marlowe was then lying, sitting near the bed that is, near the bed and with the front part of his body near the table and the aforesaid Nicholas Skeres and Robert Poley sitting on either side of the said Ingram in such a manner that the same Ingram Frizer in no wise could take flight; it so befell that ~~the said~~ Christopher Marlowe on a sudden and of his malice towards the ~~said~~ Ingram aforethought, was at his back, and with the same dagger ~~the said Christopher~~ Marlowe then and there maliciously gave the ~~aforesaid~~ Ingram two wounds on his head of the length of two inches and of the depth of a quarter of an inch; whereupon the said Ingram, in fear of being slain, and sitting in the manner aforesaid between the said Nicholas Skeres and Robert Poley so that he could not in any wise get away, in his own defence and for the saving of his life, then and there struggled with ~~the said~~ Christopher Marlowe to get from him his dagger ~~aforesaid~~; in which affray ~~the same~~ Ingram could not get away from ~~the said~~ Christopher Marlowe, and so it befell in that affray that ~~the said~~ Ingram, in defence of his life, with the dagger aforesaid of the value of 12 d, gave ~~the said~~ Christopher then and there a mortal wound over his right eye of the depth of two inches and the width of one inch; of which mortal wound the ~~aforesaid~~ Christopher Marlowe then and there instantly died.

The Queen's pardon of Ingram Frizer followed:

. . . We therefore, moved by piety, have pardoned the same Ingram Frizer the breach of our peace which pertains to us against the said Ingram for the death above mentioned and grant to him our firm peace Provided:

nevertheless that the right remain in our Court if anyone should wish to complain of him concerning the death above mentioned.

In testimony etc.,

Witnesseth the Queen at Kew
on the 28th day of June.

There is no doubt, the record is genuine. It is the coroner's official report. It is stamped with the integrity of the Queen's royal stamp and signed with her royal hand.

It is on this document that the truth of Christopher Marlowe's murder must hang. Certainly, we are entitled to demand that this report of Marlowe's death be indisputable.

Now, then, did William Danby, Coroner to the Household

of our Lady the Queen, seek and conscientiously state the unvarnished truth in his account of Marlowe's murder?

Let us examine his own testimony. The following are some of the discrepancies that the report seemed to have corrected:

The date of the murder: the parish Burial Register gave the date of Marlowe's slaying as "1st June, 1593," whereas it actually occurred two days earlier—May 30, 1593.

The murderer's name: The Burial Register recorded it as *Francis Archer.* The true name was *Ingram Frizer.* An astonishing correction, this.

The motive: it was not over Marlowe's "lewd love," or a "lewd wench"; it was due to a quarrel "about the payment of the sum of pence, that is, the reckoning." We don't know the sum involved.

The setting: there is no evidence that the murder took place in a tavern: the Coroner's report states that it happened in "a room in the house of a certain Eleanor Bull, Widow."

The swift-flowing events that preceded the murder.

Marlowe was lying on, or sitting near, a bed. Frizer was sitting at a table with his back toward Marlowe, between his two friends, Skeres and Poley. Marlowe, in his position, faced Frizer's back. Marlowe abruptly seized Frizer's dagger, and with "malice aforethought" gave Frizer "two wounds in the head of the length of two inches and of the depth of a quarter of an inch." Whereupon Frizer, sitting between Skeres and Poley, "so that he could not in any wise get away," and "in fear of being slain," and "in his own defence and for the saving of his life," then and there struggled with Marlowe to "get from him his dagger." Frizer "could not get away" from Marlowe. So "it befell in that affray" that Frizer, "in defence of his life and with the dagger of the value of 12 pence" gave Marlowe "then and there a mortal wound over his right eye of the depth of two inches and the width of one inch, of which mortal wound Marlowe then and there instantly died."

Let us take a closer look, now, at what transpired on the morning of the crime—May 30, 1593.

The coroner's report informs us that "Christopher Marlowe, there lying dead," in the company of Ingram Frizer, Nicholas Skeres and Robert Poley, at about ten o'clock in the morning of May 30, 1953, "met together in a room in the house of a certain Eleanor Bull, widow, and there passed the time together and dined and after dinner [i.e., the noonday meal] were in quiet sort together [a lovely phrase, but somehow not indicative of the Marlowe we have investigated so far in this argument—Christopher Marlowe was anything but a quiet fellow] . . . and walked in the garden belonging to the said house until the 6th hour after noon of the same day [i.e., 6:00 P. M.] and then returned from the said garden to the room aforesaid and there together and in company supped; and after supper"—around 7:00 or 8:00 P. M. presumably—Frizer and Marlowe engaged in a quarrel over the payment of "the sum of pence," that is, the reckoning.

Then the murder.

Let us return to Coroner Danby. His report stated that Frizer, Skeres, Poley and Marlowe, on May 30, at 10 A. M., met in room of Eleanor Bull, in Deptford, just across the Thames. The day was a quiet one, and the atmosphere suggested by the quaint legalisms that make up Danby's Report is almost studious. The men walked and talked in a garden. After dinner, a quarrel began over the reckoning. In their room, where they had retired for an after-dinner talk, the quarrel over the dinner check waxed loud for a few moments.

And then, some solution probably having been found, the men were quiet.

Marlowe sat, or lay, on a bed. Frizer was sitting at or near a table with his back to Marlowe. Skeres and Poley were seated on either side of Frizer at the table, so that "Ingram Frizer in no wise could take flight." All three men were sitting at the table with their backs to Marlowe; Frizer sat between (to repeat) Skeres and Poley.

A strange picture, indeed. An odd foursome for an after-dinner talk, even an acrimonious one. Three men sitting at a table (probably on a long bench), with their backs to a third man lying on a bed.

Then Marlowe, acting on impulse, snatched Frizer's dagger (which was "at his back"—a strange place for the sort of man that Frizer was to keep his weapon. He would have been at a disadvantage in any brawl, if he had had to twist himself around to reach his dagger sheathed behind him) and stabbed Frizer, giving him two wounds in the head (two inches long and a quarter of an inch deep).

Two insignificant scalp wounds, made by a good steel dagger, wielded by an infuriated man, who stabbed downward with all the power of his body!

Frizer, with remarkable control under the circumstances, must have sat frozen while Marlowe stabbed him twice.

Further, Marlowe's robotlike precision must have been marvelous to behold—since both wounds were identical. He must have struck his patient adversary twice with the same force, in the same way.

After this, Frizer must have lost patience with Marlowe's unfriendly exhibition. Having sat quietly and with equanimity through two dagger thrusts, he decided that the time had come to act. As the coroner tells us, Frizer, "in fear of being slain," although he was "sitting . . . between Skeres and Poley so that he could not in any wise get away, in his own defence and for the saving of his life," struggled with Marlowe to disarm him.

And what of Frizer's two friends, Skeres and Poley? What were they doing while Frizer sat quiet through the two dagger thrusts?

These two gentlemen must have decided to join the conspiracy of immobility. They sat, frozen and patient, in their seats while Frizer and Marlowe battled it out. The death brawl eddied about them while they did not budge. They did not move an inch.

Imbued, no doubt, with the English spirit of fair play, Skeres and Poley did not in any way try to stop the brawl.

Coroner Danby: "And so it befell in that affray that the said Frizer, in defence of his life, with the dagger aforesaid . . . gave the said Christopher then and there a mortal wound over his right eye of the depth of two inches and the width of one inch," from which wound Marlowe "then and there instantly died."

It is curious, indeed, that men of action (and we know that Frizer, Skeres, and Poley were such) should have spent a day in contemplative discussion with a dangerous intellectual like Marlowe.

It is curious to speculate as to how Frizer ultimately did manage to retrieve his dagger from Marlowe, and finally to kill him. Nowhere does the coroner elaborate this point.

What were the four men actually doing on May 30, 1593, between 10:00 A. M. and nightfall?

Who instigated the meeting? There was nothing in common between these bullyboys and Marlowe. Why should they want to meet at all?

What was Eleanor Bull's house: a tavern, a brothel, a boardinghouse? Did she know the men in question?

Since there was a heated quarrel between Marlowe and Frizer over the reckoning, why was Frizer (a man of action, remember) sitting with his back toward the excitable Marlowe, his dagger in inviting and totally ridiculous position behind his back? In today's terms, it is as though a western gunslinger, after a violent argument with a fellow at a bar, turned his back on his enemy, wearing his six-shooter at his back, its handle pointed invitingly toward his foe.

Again, how could Frizer have swung around after Marlowe wounded him on his headtop, if, as Coroner Danby states, Skeres and Poley prevented him from getting out of their way?

Why didn't Skeres and Poley call for help or seek out Mrs.

Bull, either during the brawl or after the murder? Three men against one, remember. Couldn't they have knocked Marlowe cold, without killing him? What did they do to prevent the murder? Who engaged the room at Mrs. Bull's? Who paid for it? Was she called as a witness?

Did the coroner know whether Frizer, Skeres, and Poley were friends? Did Mrs. Bull make an outcry of any kind (she must certainly have heard the terrific noise) before or after the death struggle? Who summoned the constabulary? Who summoned Coroner Danby?

These and other questions are not answered by Danby's recitation. Therefore, on what I consider legitimate grounds, the report must support investigation.

Now, the coroner swore that Marlowe "then and there instantly died" from the blow inflicted by Frizer. It can be stated that it is an impossibility for a human being to die instantly from such a wound as the coroner described in his report.

In due time, I shall elaborate on this.

Can we be convinced beyond doubt that the coroner sought "the truth, the whole truth, and nothing but the truth"? I doubt it. Coroner Danby obtained evidence solely from Nicholas Skeres and Robert Poley, both known friends of Ingram Frizer's. Danby must have been both credulous and inefficient not to have asked the most basic questions of the witnesses, before writing his report of the homicide. Surely Frizer's plea of "self-defence" must have caused Danby embarrassment.

But why was Danby so credulous? And who caused the name "Francis Archer" to appear in the Deptford Church Burial Register instead of the name of the actual murderer, Ingram Frizer?

Is it not possible that Coroner Danby was acting under instructions?

Let us take a closer look for the minute at Frizer, Skeres, and Poley—the murderer and his friends.

Each of them, before May 30, 1953, and for years afterwards, was in the employ of Marlowe's friend and protector, Sir Thomas Walsingham.

Each had done work for the Lord of Scadbury Park in Chislehurst and for his Lady. Each of these bullies had an odorous reputation—Miss Eugenie De Kalb, literary researcher, has revealed that Ingram Frizer, Marlowe's murderer, was a notorious swindler, through whose machinations his employers, Sir Thomas and Lady Walsingham, often profited.

Frizer was the Elizabethan version of today's con man. He was commonly used as a foil in a series of fraudulent litigations. Up to almost the very day of the Deptford murder records show him associated with the Walsinghams. Almost exactly a month after Marlowe's death (June 29, 1953)—in fact the very day following Elizabeth's Royal Pardon—Frizer resumed employment with Walsingham and proceeded to help him in a commercial transaction that was as illegal as it was cunningly conceived.

One day, therefore, after he was freed by the Queen, the murderer of his close friend and protégé was rehired by Walsingham.

Frizer continued to live in Wasingham's house—Scadbury Park—until at least four years after his crime (1597). During this time he worked closely with his master as "dummy" behind many real estate affairs in which Lady Walsingham featured. In numerous leases granted by the crown in "reversion" to Ingram Frizer, they are skillfully manipulated so that profit accrues only to her.

Frizer's association with the Walsinghams extends well into the reign of James I, who became king upon Elizabeth's death in 1603. Twenty years after the Deptford incident

Frizer was still employed by Christopher Marlowe's patron, Sir Thomas Walsingham.

Nicholas Skeres is just as unsavory a character. His dossier identifies him as a "robber" and a "cutpurse." He is habitually in and out of jail. His relationship with Walsingham consists in his having given assistance to Sir Thomas and to Robert Poley in the famous Babington Catholic conspiracy directed against the Queen. Skeres is listed as a spy in the service of the government, in 1589. He is involved, as Frizer's accomplice, in a swindle undertaken for the benefit of Sir Thomas Walsingham.

The worst of the three is Robert Poley. Like Skeres, he was sentenced to prison at more or less regular intervals, often for the purpose of informing on other prisoners. He was one of the more able of the government spies. He was dispatched on several important missions abroad. Poley was also a convicted adulterer. He was engaged in espionage and counter-espionage in both England and the Continent, and was one of the spies who ferreted out the Babington plot. Skeres and Sir Thomas were, as has been noted, associated with Poley in that enterprise. A letter which survives Poley tells of procuring "Mr. Thomas Walsingham for my secret recourse to Mr. Secretary" (Sir Francis Walsingham, Secretary of State).

Strangest of all is that in May, 1953, Poley left England for The Hague on government business. On the day of Marlowe's murder—May 30, 1593—he returned from Holland with secret information for Sir Thomas Walsingham, and from that meeting with his employer he went to Eleanor Bull's house in Deptford—there to meet with Marlowe, Ingram Frizer, and Nicholas Skeres.

It seems simple enough to conclude that someone gave Poley orders to go to Eleanor Bull's establishment—else, why should he have done so? Certainly he could not, in that age of laborious communication, have arranged for the meeting while abroad. The only explanation is that he received his orders, pressing orders, to do what he did.

As for the giver of those orders—the chain of evidence encircles Walsingham and does not let him go.

For the moment, back to the inquest. It took place on June 1. We also know that sixteen jurors, or witnesses, required by law, were present in the room on June 1 where they ". . . viewed the body of Christopher Marlowe there lying dead and slain." The jurors agreed with the coroner's verdict of "murder in self-defence."

Who were these sixteen witnesses? The report lists their names. They have been identified as either tradesmen, servingmen, or farmers. Yet there is something remarkable about the presence of these sixteen men in Eleanor Bull's house.

The murder occurred on the night of May 30. Ingram Frizer "neither fled nor withdrew himself" (a sign of a clean conscience on the part of the murderer) and therefore nothing was done with the body or about the crime until the following day—May 31.

We don't know to which authority the crime was first reported. Someone in power knew that the local Deptford coroner would not have jurisdiction over the stabbing, since the murder took place within the royal "verge." The expression referred to the law stating that wherever her Majesty was holding court her personal sovereignty extended within twelve miles of where she was staying. Since we know that the Queen was at either Kew or Greenwich at the time of the slaying, Deptford certainly fell within the royal prerogative.

Marlowe's murder, therefore, necessitated the services of the crown's coroner, William Danby, whose authority superseded that of the local coroner. Since there was ceremony involved in the calling of the crown coroner (the age was a ceremonious one, a time of earnest, childlike, and precious complexities), it could not possibly have been until midafternoon of May 31 at the earliest that Coroner Danby arrived at Eleanor Bull's establishment.

In the meantime, sixteen jurors would have to be impaneled to witness and listen to the testimony presented. They arrived at Deptford the following day, June 1—all sixteen of them.

And there lies a remarkable fact. These sixteen men arrived, all of them, on time. This in an age when there was no telephone, telegraphy, wireless, train, or automobile. An age whose communication consisted of horse or foot.

How could it have been possible to summon sixteen citizens from their homes in neighboring villages between the daylight hours of the afternoon of May 31 and June 1, and have them convene in Deptford?

How was it possible to conduct the inquest, with its cumbersome formality, question witnesses, swear the depositions, and complete the inquisition itself? This, mind you, in an age when all court testimony was written by hand, without the help of Pitman or Gregg, an age enamored of all the pompous trappings of the law?

And after all this time-consuming process, Marlowe's body, with at least a minimum of formality, had to be moved to St. Nicholas Churchyard, before being interred in its anonymous grave—and all this on the very same afternoon of June 1, since the Burial Register specifically states that Marlowe was entombed on that day.

It would have been something very like a miracle to have accomplished all this within the space of eighteen hours of daylight. A miracle which mocks itself.

Perhaps it might have been done if Marlowe's murder had been a special case, but it was not. There was no reason for undue haste; everything was open and aboveboard.

The coroner, in his summing up, was careful to insert in his report the testimony of the sixteen jurors, writing: "And further the said Jurors say upon their oath that the said Frizer, after the slaying aforesaid, perpetrated and done by him in the manner and form aforesaid, neither fled nor withdrew himself." If the murderer was in no hurry, why should the law be?

There is an explanation for this bravado, of course. Fleeing from the scene of a homicide was at the time a powerful admission of guilt. Frizer wished to make clear that he was no hit-and-run murderer. He succeeded, obviously, in impressing the panel and the coroner.

The coroner's report insists that "Frizer in no wise could take flight" and that "he could not in any wise get away from Christopher Marlowe"; and that only "in his own defence and for the saving of his life" was he forced to kill Marlowe. A brief understanding of Elizabethan law makes the coroner's report more illuminating than it might otherwise be. While "self-defence," when proved, is sufficient in itself to win acquittal on a murder charge, it must also be shown that the defendant involved had no means of escaping his assailant, and that only when his own life lay imperiled was he forced to resort to taking the life of his assailant.

Knowing this, it is possible to judge Danby's report for what it was—as perfect a document for eventually acquitting a murderer as Danby, with all his legal acumen, could devise.

On June 1, 1593, Danby presented his findings to the Court of Chancery. They were accepted on face value, without further investigation.

On June 15, 1593, two weeks later, a "writ of Certiorari" issued out of Chancery. Ingram Frizer was to all intents and purposes a free man. He waited for the formality of the Queen's official pardon, which was granted him on June 28, 1593.

Danby's report had done its work well.

The following day, June 29, Frizer was back at Scadbury Park, working with Marlowe's great friend and protector,

Sir Thomas Walsingham, on business of personal and financial importance to the lord of the manor.

In 1925 the coroner's report was discovered. It should have made conclusive Marlowe's murder. Instead, it has created more genuine mistrust in Marlowe's supposed death than if it had never been found.

It would reasonably seem that the report is filled with incongruities; that its very detail, detail which makes it a precious document historically, casts doubt on its veracity. Certainly, an objective mind can be forgiven for summing up Danby's report as a patent fraud.

Might not Walsingham, assisted perhaps by Marlowe, have plotted the murder? There is certainly a possibility that they did and, as we shall later see, William Shakespeare knew part of the text of the inquest.

But back to Danby's report. For, instead of a record of death, it is possible to make the report yield a certificate of life.

Marlowe's death would so yield. You will remember that, in the report, Christopher Marlowe of a "wound over his right eye of the depth of two inches and the width of one inch . . . then and there instantly died." Evidently, Danby carefully examined the wound; measured it, with scrupulous attention.

But can a human being "instantly die" of a wound such as the coroner so meticulously described? Modern medical science says no. In a book called *The Assassination of Christopher Marlowe,* Dr. Tannenbaum, a medical doctor who, before his recent death, specialized in psychoanalysis and was a first-rate Elizabethan scholar, went on record to say that Marlowe's death from the wound described was a medical impossibility. Instant death, Tannenbaum insisted, could not possibly result from a dagger thrust above the right eye, measuring two inches deep and one inch wide. He wrote that one so wounded could linger on for days in a state of prolonged coma, eventually followed by death; but that death would not, in the circumstances specified, result "then and there instantly."

In support of his thesis, Dr. Tannenbaum gathered the written testimony of several of the most noted neurosurgeons in the U.S.A. and, with their documented and technical opinions to buttress his argument, he printed their confirmed evidence. All the specialists consulted agreed with Dr. Tannenbaum.

But Tannenbaum wrote his book in 1928. The advance in brain surgery that drove forward under the impetus of World War II has in the interim rendered even Tannenbaum's denial obsolete.

Surgeons of our time, in their efforts to explore, and therefore to heal, have removed whole sections of the human brain, with no serious physical danger to the patient. Present-day surgeons maintain that a dagger thrust into the head of some six or seven inches in depth, and two inches in width—straight back into the occipital lobe—need not result in death at all. The patient might well have every prospect of living on, though mentally impaired.

Death, therefore, could not result from even a far more serious injury than the one from which the coroner stated Marlowe had "then and there instantly died."

What do other critics and scholars think of the report of Marlowe's murder? Here are a few opinions, gathered from experts in the life and works of Marlowe, specialists in Elizabethan literature. No better informed authorities on Marlowe exist. They are all Shakespearean conservatives: they all believe that William Shakespeare wrote the plays attributed to him; they have no ax to grind, at least not as regards this argument; here is what they tell us:

Leslie Hotson (in his book, *The Death of Christopher Marlowe*):

[One course, of two] open about Marlowe's death . . . is to suppose that Frizer, Poley and Skeres, after the slaying and in order to save Frizer's life on a plea of self-defense concocted a lying account of Marlowe's behavior to which they swore at the Inquest and with which they deceived the jury. . . . [This] seems to me a possible . . . view of the case.

C. F. Tucker Brooke (in his *The Reputation of Christopher Marlowe*):

Concerning the manner of Marlowe's death, his acquaintances maintain a reticence which is baffling to biographers.

Frederick S. Boas (in his biography, *Christopher Marlowe*):

It is surprising that the references to the event [i.e., Marlowe's murder] in the years immediately following should have been so scanty and so curiously vague or misleading. Mistakes began on the very day of the Inquest. . . . Nor is there any indication in the churchyard of the place of the grave. . . . Gabriel Harvey thought Marlowe died of the plague in 1593! In his "Gorgon or the Wonderful Year"—September 18, 1593 —the line, "the great disease sternly struck home the stroke" must surely imply Marlowe's death from the plague! The more Harvey's references are considered the more enigmatic they become. [Summing up, Marlowe's death to Professor Boas "is a puzzle."]

Dr. Samuel A. Tannenbaum (in his book, *The Assassination of Christopher Marlowe*):

The Coroner's Inquest was a perfunctory matter. His story cannot be accepted as a faithful account of what actually transpired. . . . The Coroner was influenced by certain powers not to enquire too curiously into Marlowe's violent death. . . . Here was an excellent trio [i.e., Frizer, Poley, and Skeres] for a contrived murder. . . . Marlowe's death was premeditated assassination. No physician was called to dress Ingram Frizer's wounds which were probably too slight to require medical attention. . . . Frizer's wounds are so curious a phenomenon as to warrant the assumption they were self-inflicted. . . . The Coroner's tale of Marlowe's end is not a true account of what happened.

John Bakeless (in *The Tragical History of Christopher Marlowe*):

> The discovery of the documents relating to Marlowe's death raises almost as many questions as it answers. . . . Doubts persistently arise about [it] . . . The fact that Marlowe was at this time held by the Privy Council . . . makes matters still more suspicious. . . . One wonders whether he may not have been killed deliberately. . . . Frizer probably owed his easy escape to the Walsinghams for whom he was transacting business the very next day [i.e., after his pardon by Queen Elizabeth on the charge of murder]. . . . There is something queer about the whole episode.

John H. Ingram (biographer and critic of Marlowe's *Works* in an article in the *Universal Review*):

> An unfathomable mystery envelops Marlowe's last days on earth.

Contrast these considered remarks about the mystery of Marlowe's death with the statement of the most respected scholar in Shakespearean study—Sir Edmund K. Chambers. His statement about the life and lack of evidence of the education of William Shakespeare bears reexamination here:

> After all the careful scrutiny of clues and all the patient balancing of possibilities, the last word of a self-respecting scholarship can only be that of nescience [i.e., the state of not knowing; ignorance, due to the nature of the human mind or of external things].

It is nescience then—the state of not knowing—that characterizes the consensus about Marlowe's death. It is nescience that characterizes all we know of the most important period in the life of William Shakespeare.

What can self-respecting scholarship make of this?

There is an answer to the jigsaw puzzle. It is provided by the march of historical events themselves, and by them alone.

It is not, decidedly, wishful thinking. Rather, it is an inexorable, though circumstantial, conclusion.

Christopher Marlowe was not slain, as alleged. He lived on to write the works known as William Shakespeare's.

The reason there is doubt about Shakespeare's literary life is simple: we know tragically little about William Shakespeare the author because (1) until his name appeared as author of the poems and plays he had been insignificant as a person and as a force and (2) he had had no reputation as a poet or playwright because he had never written the Works which we so far know as his.

Even among the most orthodox circles, where the scent of formal scholarship hangs heavy in the air, doubts invade the quiet rooms and disturb the concentration of the Marlowe critic, the Shakespearean scholar, as he tries, without much success, to make light where there is darkness.

Without apology, therefore, let me try to reconstruct Marlowe's assassination and his afterlife, as it must have taken place, no matter how bizarre it may appear. It is the only answer that brings into focus the jigsaw puzzle.

Let us return to a few days before May 29, 1593, the date that Richard Baines dispatched his deadly charge of heresy and treason against Marlowe to the Privy Council. Marlowe had already been arrested at his patron's home in Chislehurst, where he had been living at the time Thomas Kyd first accused him of atheism.

Marlowe, between May 20 and May 29, 1593, was free only under bail. Thomas Walsingham was close to powerful men in the government; not the least of these was Francis Walsingham, his cousin, who before his death in 1590 had been Secretary of State and member of the Privy Council. This is all documented. There is no doubt that Thomas Walsingham's influence in high places, made secure in the days of his brother's power, outlived the latter's death.

Walsingham's friends, especially those involved in the

government, would have been aware of his patronage of, and interest in, Christopher Marlowe. Publishers had referred to it.

Further, these men might well have been aware of Walsingham's true relationship to Marlowe. Homosexuality could be hidden, of course; but chances are that Walsingham, with the Elizabethan aristocrat's disdain of the moral law and order which was so egregiously preached to the masses, would hardly have tried to hide his vices.

Powerful connections, therefore, Walsingham surely had— but they were not powerful enough to stop the doom that threatened Walsingham's atheist lover. He would, though, have been informed well in advance of the ever-increasing danger into which Marlowe was rushing headlong, carried along by his own imprudence. Before Baines's note was delivered to the Privy Council, he must have known of it—and of the end that it heralded for Marlowe.

The Watson-Bradley duel must have been in Marlowe's mind, as it had been ever since its occurrence. Perhaps he brooded about it; and most probably, he talked of it; mentioned that Watson's defense had been "murder in self-defense" and that he had got off scot-free. What would work for one murderer would work for another.

The scheme developed slowly. Marlowe was to be "murdered." The charges against him would vanish with his "death." And, paradoxically, his life would be saved.

The world leaves its dead in peace.

Queen Elizabeth would be at Kew, or Greenwich. The homicide would take place within the "verge"; that 12-mile area which bowed to the crown's jurisdiction and superseded all local authority. This was of importance, since Walsingham's influence with the Queen's servants would be the underpinning of the conspiracy.

The murder would have to be valid—beyond suspicion.

Its legality must be suspicion-tight. The plan must be carefully drawn up.

The situation is irresistible. Picture to yourself the home of Sir Thomas Walsingham. In one of the studies on the second floor, surrounded by the brown leather and oak paneling of quiet reflection, the two men sit, their faces averted from the fire that crackles in the fireplace. It would be late at night—perhaps nine o'clock. In a world that bedded early and rose with the sun, this would be late indeed. The two talk quietly, Walsingham's heavy tones belling with authority, while the high-pitched voice of Marlowe answers him. Ground to a keen edge, this young man; exacerbated with tension and with fear. The conversation must have gone on far into the night. Recriminations must have flown thick and fast—mostly from Walsingham, one imagines, who would not like the situation one iota. Perhaps tempers snapped, late in the firelit evening; but out of all the tension the plan evolved. They sat until late, these two, planning the faked death of Marlowe.

The day dawns bright and warm. At Scadbury Park, Walsingham talks to his servant Ingram Frizer. It is a strange twosome; a trust founded on distrust. Nicholas Skeres is there too, in the background, not too bright, but useful in an emergency. They are to kill a man—any man—and will be well paid.

The money bag flashes on the table, its coarse leather mouth spills sovereigns, and Skeres and Frizer scoop up the first installment of their pay. All they know is that they must kill. The less they know the better.

Skeres and Frizer are not worried.

They have killed before. They will kill again. Life is cheap in sixteenth-century England.

Poley is at The Hague, but if he returns in time he will be hastened on to assist the two.

Now for the place. Since the plot has been revealed to

Danby, the Queen's Coroner (who has been well paid to keep a secret which, if he revealed it, would mean his death), it must be a village "within the verge," where Danby's authority will extend. Deptford comes to mind. It is sufficiently close to Chislehurst, so that Walsingham can oversee his developing plot. It is a dock-front area. Ships from all nations tie up there, and foreigners crowd the city streets, and brawl in the local taverns. Sir Francis Drake's *Golden Hind* is at anchor there, and the curious of the world flock to see the great ship.

Deptford is an unsavory water-front district—ideal for Walsingham's purposes. It will be easy to select a victim among the strangers in the port—preferably a foreigner— perhaps an Italian or a Spaniard. He would be unknown to the inhabitants. And there would be no motive for the crime. Walsingham knows, as do his two servants, that an unmotivated crime—a completely unmotivated crime—in which the murderer has never before seen his victim is the perfect crime.

But where is the assassination to take place? Not in a tavern or a hostel—but in an inconspicuous place, a private house preferably. Frizer, who is a rogue, and who chases women, knows of one.

The date of the murder: as soon as possible. Wednesday, May 30, is agreed upon.

The conspiracy is set. The two assassins gather up their gold and leave for Deptford.

At Scadbury Park the plans for Marlowe's escape mature. He must leave the country. The chance that someone would recognize him after the murder is one that cannot be taken. Not only Marlowe's life, Walsingham's and his accomplices lives are in peril. The night before the Deptford murder the dramatist, disguised, will take horse to Dover and embark across the Channel to France. His manuscripts and private writings will be left in Walsingham's hands. Among them is the poem *Venus and Adonis,* registered six weeks earlier with the Stationers Company.

Marlowe packs his books—his Holinshed, his Halle, his Ovid, Seneca and Virgil. He will continue to write wherever he is. Communication with Walsingham would be arranged at a later date.

The two men say good-bye. The morning of the 30th dawns.

Marlowe is already in Dover—a "dead" man fleeing to France. Frizer and Skeres are in Deptford. Early that morning they stroll the town. They have little to say to each other; Skeres is angry—he cannot drink, and yet around him the sack, the strong ale, the canary flow like water. He is anxious to spot his victim. They find him in a narrow street.

At first the man is wary, and ready to fight. But Frizer suggests a drink and offers to pay for it. He clinks Walsingham's gold suggestively in his pocket, and the three turn into a tavern.

The conversation, led by Frizer, turns to women. He mentions conquests. The sailor needs little prodding. He could do with a wench, after three weeks on board ship. Frizer winks at him. He knows a place—been there often—Eleanor Bull's house; an accommodating widow, who can shut her left eye when her right is dazzled by gold.

By the time the men arrive at Eleanor Bull's house they are reasonably sober. The fresh morning air has done its work. In the small bedroom of the house they drink.

There's a knock on the door, and Walsingham enters, with Poley, disheveled from his long hard ride. He declines wine. No name is mentioned. He looks once, quickly, at the drunken guests, and nods perhaps. He leaves as silently as he has come. Poley remains.

The drinking continues. But the sailor, who by now has stretched himself comfortably on the plank bed, is too drunk to see. The three murderers gulp down their wine and call for more. They are half drunk themselves. The air of the room, reeking with wine and the mingled odors of unwashed bodies, thickens with purpose.

The three men are waiting; waiting. Even they cannot stab in cold blood.

Then the tension snaps; the murderers throw themselves upon their guest, and in a minute the sailor is dead of stab wounds. And Marlowe is officially "dead."

8

ON June 1, the body was removed to St. Nicholas Church, some streets away, and there buried in an unknown and unmarked grave.

Ingram Frizer had, of course, been taken into prearranged custody.

Under Coroner Danby's order, the vicar of the Deptford church recorded the death as "Christopher Marlowe, slain by Francis Archer"—a name which Danby must have picked out of the blue.

In London, the word has spread that Christopher Marlowe, athiest and playmaker, is dead of the plague. The city doesn't much care at the time; the people are busy with their own dead; the uncounted, swollen thousands that heap the melancholy death carts.

The Baines-Kyd charges of atheism and treason against Marlowe are impotent now. Marlowe's friends mourn him. The files of the Privy Council are closed. Marlowe has escaped the stake.

. . . The figure on the Channel ship watches the tender outlines of the French coast as they emerge out of the morning mist, purple and gold in the rising sun. . . .

This is, of course, only a fictionalized approximation of how the Marlowe-Shakespeare fraud began. But it must have happened somewhat in this way.

What follows now is precisely what the records, fortified by documentary evidence, reveal after May 30, 1593.

Thirteen days pass, and the Court of Chancery accepts Coroner Danby's version of the Deptford homicide as a "murder in self-defence." Ingram Frizer is freed, even ahead of schedule. He waits for the technicality of the Queen's pardon, which arrives with unusual promptness two weeks later—June 28, 1593.

There is nothing in the records of Elizabethan times that compares with the swiftness with which Ingram Frizer won his release. By way of contrast, Thomas Watson (in the brawl that involved Marlowe, and in which William Bradley was killed, who was arrested on a charge of murder and pleaded "self-defence," languished in prison for five months before regaining his freedom.

Coroner Danby filed his report. The record was placed in the archives. And it was not seen again until 332 years later, in 1925.

On June 29, 1593—one day after he received the Queen's royal pardon—Ingram Frizer was living at the home of Sir Thomas Walsingham—engaged in a thieving operation, the benefits of which went directly into the pockets of Walsingham and his formidable wife. Skeres and Poley, similarly, resumed their service with Walsingham.

Four months later—in September 1593—the name "William Shakespeare" made its appearance in a book, *Venus and Adonis,* a poem anonymously registered April 18, 1593. This was the first time Shakespeare's name ever appeared on any work of any kind.

9

WHERE did Marlowe flee to after his escape from England and death? The question is, of course, unanswerable, in the light of direct evidence. But one can conjecture:

I believe he went to France, and shortly thereafter to Italy. Writing must have helped him in his exile. I believe, too, that he never kept out of touch with Walsingham; that they communicated regularly; and that he sent his friend and patron, at intervals, every play and poem that he completed.

Every student of literature knows that the sonnet is the most personal and revealing of all forms of self-expression. It is the literary confessional itself. Listen to the Shakespeare Sonnet 48:

> How careful was I when I took my way
> Each trifle under truest bars to thrust
> That to my use, it might unused stay
> From hands of falsehood, in sure ward of trust!

The word "trifle" was a gesture of humility used in describing a literary work, play, or poem. The First Folio plays were actually called "these trifles" by John Heming and Henry Condell in their dedication of the 1623 volume to the Earls of Pembroke and Montgomery.

Walsingham felt sure that he would receive before long more manuscripts from his exiled protégé. What was he to do with these "trifles" that he held in trust?

(1) He must have concluded that Marlowe's handwriting

was too well known around London, where playhouses and publishers owned the manuscripts of his previously written dramas. It would be dangerous indeed for any of the newer plays to find their way into hands that would immediately recognize the handwriting as Marlowe's. Not to speak of Walsingham's danger. For Walsingham, if the truth were told, would have been guilty, not only of murder, but of suborning the Queen's coroner. His head would be lopped off without much ado.

(2) He must have felt, after reading Marlowe's work, that it should be published. Not only did England deserve the works in question, but it would be truly cruel to the exiled dramatist to hold his writing in escrow for a dim and uncertain future, a future in which both Walsingham and Marlowe might be dead. Walsingham must have realized that the manuscripts were dangerous—but only, of course, as long as they were written in Marlowe's handwriting and signed with Marlowe's name.

He must have come to the logical conclusion. Walsingham was no fool. He had kept his head not only on his shoulders, through an era that was unkind to such protuberances, but even above water. He was to keep afloat in the political stream for many years to come. No, he was not naïve or foolish. He decided to have Marlowe's manuscripts copied.

For this purpose he needed a professional scrivener, one he could trust. He would retain the originals, hiding them safely, once they had been copied, from the sight of the world. He would go to the London playhouses, and seek out some obscure actor, who would, for ample remuneration, lend his name to any work Walsingham would bring him.

I believe that Walsingham went to London's theaters. That he found the actor he wanted: a steady, not too imaginative fellow, who could be trusted with his limited part in the enterprise and did not mind lending his name to anything as long as Walsingham's gold flowed freely.

Walsingham found this man; a man with a family; a man who could conceivably be fostered as a playwright: William Shakespeare.

I believe that Walsingham thought no time should be lost in the production of the masquerade. He must have thought a poem a wise choice with which to usher in "William Shakespeare" the "author," rather than a play. Marlowe's reputation was that of a dramatist and, therefore, such a poem would divert any possible suspicion from Marlowe as author, since no poem of Marlowe's had been published up to that time.

Since Marlowe had left a long poem "in sure ward of trust" at Scadbury Park before his departure, *Venus and Adonis* was the logical candidate for first publication.

September, 1593: *Venus and Adonis* . . . by William Shakespeare.

What, scholars will ask, of the dedication to Henry Wriothesley, the 20-year-old Earl of Southampton? It is quite probable that Walsingham himself may have deliberately written the unauthorized dedication; in an effort to make William Shakespeare as hopeful, as inconspicuous, as the other literary fledglings who vied for the potential patronage of the young earl. Walsingham must have been a careful man; his meticulousness, so apparent in his planning of the murder of Marlowe, was apparent in his preparation of the public mind for William Shakespeare, playwright.

I believe all this is the reason why *Venus and Adonis* is called "the first heir of my invention," that is, the first written work of William Shakespeare.

Significantly, after a second dedication to the Earl of Southampton, in *The Rape of Lucrece* (published in 1594), Henry Wriothsley's name disappears from Shakespeare's works, never to return. It left as abruptly as it had appeared.

Hard upon the publication of *Venus and Adonis* a flood of plays deluged the London theaters. It was only with *Love's*

Labour's Lost, five years later (1598), that Shakespeare's name was ascribed to any of these productions.

Did Christopher Marlowe return to England? I feel certain that after a few years he did, and that he lived on for the most part on the grounds of Walsingham's Scadbury estate, conceivably in disguise. Here he worked in a seclusion guaranteed by the vast parks of the estate itself.

He was free to roam the thousand-acre woods, where so many allusions to nature must have had their origin.

10

AFTER thirteen years of research I felt sure that when Marlowe fled to the Continent he continued writing, and sent the finished manuscripts by courier to his friend and patron, Walsingham. Once Walsingham received these manuscripts, he had copies made. For this he needed the services of a professional scribe.

Then, in England, I gained access to the last will and testament of Sir Thomas Walsingham. Here is an abstract of that will:

> In the name of God, Amen: the 5th day of August, 1630. I, Sir Thomas Walsingham, the elder, of Scadbury in the parish of Chislehurst, in Kent, knight. To be buried in Chislehurst Church in decent manner, without vain pomp or excess in anything. . . . All the rents, etc., of the lands, etc., in Swanton, Peckham, and Yokes, in Kent, unto my grandchild, Katherine Walsingham, until the sum of 1,000 pounds shall be raised towards a porcon [sic] for her. . . . To Sarah Cowell, my old servant, 10 pounds, and to my servant, Francis Hogan, 10 pounds. My servant Edward Thetford, 5 pounds, and my servant Thomas Moore, 20 nobles.

And then I stumbled upon this bequest:

> To Thomas Smith, scrivener, 40 shillings for a Ring. . . .

Sir Thomas died August 11, 1630.

Certainly this bequest indicated a friendship or at least personal association of some standing with a "scrivener."

The bequest of 40 shillings—a fairly substantial sum in those days—was made to purchase a ring in memory of the giver. This presupposed an intimacy between the aristocratic Walsingham and a man in trade that seemed unusual to me.

I examined numerous wills of Walsingham's era, wills which were the testaments of men in Walsingham's social and financial position—not one of them mentioned a bequest to a scrivener. It was, then, unusual for an aristocrat to mention a tradesman in his will. The relationship between Walsingham and Smith must have sprung from an unusual association.

I believe that it was Smith who copied the Marlowe documents for Walsingham to distribute to the London theaters, through the medium of William Shakespeare.

I believe that Marlowe journeyed to Italy after his escape to France. There is evidence to support my claim, literary evidence only at this time.

Many pages have been written during the centuries about Marlowe's Italianate temperament. Many reputable critics believe that he would have been more in harmony with his surroundings had he lived in the Italy of the Renaissance rather than in Elizabethan England.

For two centuries scholars have been tantalized by the idea that William Shakespeare, about 1593, might have traveled to Italy. Many of his plays, such as *Titus Andronicus, The Two Gentlemen of Verona, Romeo and Juliet,* and *The Merchant of Venice,* show a startling knowledge of Italy's geography.

Sir Edmund K. Chambers, in his massive two-volume work on William Shakespeare, reflects the attitude of most students, when he tells us:

> Much research has been devoted to a conjecture that Shakespeare spent part of this period—1592-1594—in northern Italy.

Did Christopher Marlowe, who wrote the plays ascribed to Shakespeare, settle for a while in Italy? There certainly would have been no reason for Marlowe to avoid Italy—he was alone, and banished, doubly banished. The attraction of the Queen of the World, for Italy was certainly that, in the sixteenth century most probably proved overwhelming.

11

WE have observed that the sonnet form of expression is the most revelatory of all. While I do not expect conservative Shakespearean scholars to evolve an unorthodox theory, I certainly wonder that they never perceived in *Shakespeare's Sonnets* the anguish of a pleading soul, suffocating under forced anonymity.

Interpretations given these sonnets are the most diverse of all critical literature. Some critics cluster them into sectionalism and speak of the Dark Lady behind the theme. Others admit that Shakespeare might have been homosexual, and speak of a Dark Young Man. Still others conclude that the sonnets are addressed to Cupid, to Love, to Beauty; to Youth, to Friendship, Time, and Death. An infinite variety of abstracts does not camouflage the sad fact that the *Sonnets'* dedicatee is wrapped in obscurity. The motivating force behind the poems is enigmatic.

Interpreted in the light of the Marlowe-Shakespeare imposture, these sonnets take on fresh meaning.

Only a portion of the 154 sonnets can be examined here. Yet all, or nearly all, in one way or another are linked to my thesis of authorship. The bulk of them seem to have been written after 1593—after the Deptford homicide.

Though some of them were written, as printed, in narrative sequence, most of them were not. Transposed into a probable order of succession, the *Sonnets* tell a tale of fraud, guilt, and banishment.

For our purpose we may begin with Sonnet 50, written hard upon Marlowe's journey into exile:

> How heavy do I journey on the way,
> When what I seek—my weary travel's end—
> Doth teach that ease and that repose to say,
> "Thus far the miles are measured from thy friend!"
> The beast that bears me, tired with my woe,
> Plods dully on, to bear that weight in me,
> As if by some instinct the wretch did know
> His rider lov'd not speed, being made from thee.
>
> .   .   .
>
> My grief lies onward, and my joy behind.

Sonnet 51:

> Thus can my love excuse the slow offence
> Of my dull bearer, when from thee I speed:
> From where thou art, why should I haste me thence?
>
> .   .   .
>
> O, what excuse will my poor beast then find,
> When swift extremity can seem but slow?

Sonnet 44:

> If the dull substance of my flesh were thought,
> Injurious distance should not stop my way;
> For then, despite of space, I would be brought
> From limits far remote where thou dost stay,
>
> .   .   .
>
> Upon the farthest earth removed from thee.
>
> .   .   .
>
> But that, so much of earth and water wrought
> I must attend time's leisure with my moan.

Sonnet 48:

> How careful was I when I took my way,
> Each trifle under truest bars to thrust,
> That, to my use, it might unused stay
> From hands of falsehood, in sure wards of trust.

Sonnet 27:

> Weary with toil, I haste me to my bed,
> The dear repose for limbs with travel tired;
> But then begins a journey in my head,
>
> For then my thoughts from far where I abide
> Intend a zealous pilgrimage to thee,
>
> Lo, thus, by day my limbs, by night my mind,
> For thee, and for my self, no quiet find.

Sonnet 28:

> How can I then return in happy plight,
> That am debarred the benefit of rest?
>
> How far I toil, still farther off from thee.
>
> But day doth daily draw my sorrows longer
> And night doth nightly make my grief's strength
>   seem stronger.

Sonnet 45:

> Until Life's composition be recured
> By those swift messengers returned from thee
> Who even but now come back again assured
> Of thy fair health, recounting it to me.
> This told, I joy, . . .

Sonnet 26:

> Lord of my love, to whom in vassalage
> Thy merit hath my duty strongly knit,
> To thee I send this written embassage,
> To witness duty, not to show my wit.
>
> Till whatsoever star that guides my moving
>
> To show me worthy of thy sweet respect:
> Then may I dare to boast how I do love thee,
>
> Till then, not show my head . . .

Sonnet 36:

>Let me confess that we two must be twain
>Although our undivided loves are one.

>   .   .   .

>I may not evermore acknowledge thee
>Lest my bewailed guilt should do thee shame
>Nor thou with public kindness honour me
>Unless thou take that honour from thy name.

Sonnet 74:

>But be contented: when that fell arrest
>Without all bail shall carry me away,
>My life hath in this line some interest,
>Which for memorial still with thee shall stay.
>When thou reviewest this, thou dost review
>The very part was consecrate to thee.
>The Earth can have but earth, which is his due;
>My spirit is thine, the better part of me:
>So then thou hast but lost the dregs of life,
>The prey of worms, my body being dead,
>The coward conquest of a wretch's knife
>Too base of thee to be remembered.

Sonnet 71:

>No longer mourn for me when I am dead.

>   .   .

>Nay, if you read this line, remember not
>The hand that writ it; for I love you so,
>That I in your sweet thoughts would be forgot,
>If thinking on me then should make you woe.
>O if, I say, you look upon this verse,
>When I perhaps compounded am with clay,
>Do not so much as my poor name rehearse,

>   .   .   .

>Lest the wise world should look into your moan,
>And mock you with me, after I am gone.

Sonnet 72:

>O lest the world should task you to recite

What merit lived in me, that you should love
After my death—dear love, forget me quite,

.   .   .

My name be buried where my body is,
And live no more to shame nor me nor you.

Sonnet 111:

Thence comes it that my name receives a brand.

Sonnet 112:

Which vulgar scandal stamped upon my brow

.   .   .

You so strong in my purpose bred,
That all the world besides methinks are dead.

Sonnet 17:

Who will believe my verse in time to come,

.   .   .

Though yet, Heaven knows, it is but as a tomb
Which hides your life, . . .

Sonnet 86:

Was it his spirit, by spirits taught to write
Above a mortal pitch, that struck me dead?
No, neither he, nor his compeers by night
Giving him aid, my verse astonished.
He, nor that affable familiar ghost
Which nightly gulls him with intelligence,
As victors of my silence, cannot boast . . .

Sonnet 125:

Were't aught to me I bore the canopy,
With my extern the outward honouring,
Or laid great bases for eternity?

.   .   .

Hence, thou suborned informer! a true soul
When most impeached, stands least in thy control.

Sonnet 23:

> O let my books be, then, the eloquence
>
> And dumb presagers of my speaking breast;
> Who plead for love, and look for recompense
> More than that tongue that more hath more expressed.
>
> .   .   .
>
> To hear with eyes, belongs to love's fine wit.

Sonnet 76:

> Why write I still all one, ever the same,
> And keep invention [i.e., writing] in a noted [i.e.,
>   famous] weed [i.e., disguise],
> That every word doth almost tell my name,
> Showing their birth, and where they did proceed?

Sonnet 25:

> Let those who are in favour with their stars,
> Of public honour and proud titles boast,
> Whilst I, whom fortune of such triumph bars . . .

Sonnet 29:

> When in disgrace with fortune and men's eyes,
> I all alone beweep my outcast state,
> And trouble deaf heaven with my bootless cries
> And look upon myself, and curse my fate,
>
> .   .   .
>
> Haply I think on thee—
>
> .   .   .
>
> For thy sweet love remembered such wealth brings
> That then I scorn to change my state with kings.

Sonnet 134:

> So, now I have confess'd that he is thine,
> And I myself am mortgaged to thy will,
> Myself I'll forfeit . . .
>
> .   .   .
>
> He learned but surety-like to write for me
> Under that bond that him as fast doth bind.

Sonnet 150:

> To make me give the lie to my true sight.

Sonnet 135:

> Whoever hath her wish, thou hast my will,
>
> Think all but one, and in me, that one Will.

Sonnet 136:

> If thy soul check thee that I come so near,
> Swear to thy blind soul that I was thy "Will."
>
> Then in the number let me pass untold
>
> Make but my name thy love . . .
> . . . for my name is "Will."

Sonnet 81:

> From hence your memory death cannot take,
>
> Your name from hence immortal life shall have,
> Though I, once gone, to all the world must die;
>
> Your monument shall be my gentle verse,
>
> And tongues to be, your being shall rehearse
>
> You still shall live— . . .
> . . . even in the mouths of men.

Surely we know nothing in the events of William Shakespeare's life to which a single one of these sonnets applies. It would seem as though Marlowe cries out his life, afraid to be precise, but tempted beyond his endurance to vent his anguish, somehow, in his poetry. These sonnets are the heart and soul of the Marlowe-Shakespeare mystery.

The Quarto, printed in 1609, sixteen years after the Deptford homicide, as *Shakespeare's Sonnets*, was brought out by

Thomas Thorpe, Publisher. They were, as Sir Sidney Lee, noted Shakespeare biographer, observed,

surreptitiously sent to the press.

Sir Sidney made another significant statement:

Thomas Thorpe made, in 1600, his earliest hit by bringing to light Marlowe's translation of the *First Book of Lucan*.

Might not Thorpe have similarly brought to light Marlowe's *Shakespeares Sonnets*?

Thomas Thorpe, too, composed a dedication in the Quarto which beyond all doubt has been the cause of more learned wrangling than any other dedication ever written. Whole volumes have speculated on the identity of the dedicatee, "Mr. W.H.," and just as the *Sonnets* are shrouded in a darkness that is dissolved only by the theory of Marlowe's authorship, so Mr. W.H.'s identity can be resolved in the light of the Marlowe-Shakespeare hoax. Here is the inscription:

To . the . onlie . begetter . of
these . insuing . sonnets .
Mr. W. H. all . happinesse .
And . that . eternitie .
promised .
by .
Our . ever-living . Poet .
wisheth .
The . well-wishing .
Adventurer . in .
Setting .
Forth .

Who was this Mr. W.H.? Some believe that the initials are those of Henry Wriothesley, Earl of Southampton. Though his initials are, obviously, H.W., this barrier is surmounted by stating that the printer in setting his type transposed the initials in error from H.W. to W.H.

Sir Sidney Lee disagrees (as do many scholars) and calls

the above attribution "reckless." On plausible grounds he believes that no one in Elizabethan England would have had the temerity to address an earl, in the front-ranks of the peerage, unceremoniously as "Mr." Certainly, no stationer-tradesman such as Thorpe would have dared such a breach of conduct, one which would have been severely dealt with under law.

Therefore, Sir Sidney Lee concluded that it was impossible for Thorpe to have referred to Henry Wriothesley as "Mr." even if the initials had been transposed during the setting of the type.

Thorpe called "Mr. W.H." the "onlie begetter" of the *Sonnets*—which commonly means their inspirer. Whoever Mr. W.H. was, he must have been someone close to the poet—someone intimately associated with the author.

In the light of my argument, who was close to Marlowe? Thomas Walsingham of course. Friend, patron, lover, mingled with Marlowe's very existence at every turn, arbiter of Marlowe's fate, only Walsingham qualifies as Mr. W.H.

Here are my reasons:

Marlowe's patron was knighted by Queen Elizabeth in August of 1597. Knighthood was, and is today, lowest in the hierarchy of royal distinction. The title is not hereditary. Its bestowal places the recipient only one rank above the commoner.

It would certainly be no serious infraction of etiquette if Walsingham had been addressed as "Mr." And Thorpe, as we shall later see, might have valid reasons for printing the dedication as he did.

How does W.H. apply to Walsingham? Hyphening proper names was an accepted practice in Renaissance England. Surnames were often split into syllables. For example, dramatist Anthony Munday was sometimes written as Mun-day; historian Raphael Holinshed, as Holin-shed; Lord Burleigh as Bur-leigh; Archbishop Cranmer as Cran-mer. The name Marlowe has also been written as Mar-low; and even the surname Shakespeare was often rendered as Shake-speare.

Many of the Quarto plays, in point of fact, contain the name William Shake-speare. In the memorial verses contained in the First Folio of 1623, no less than five references are made to the name "Shake-speare."

Walsingham's name was often, and similarly, hyphened—Walsing-ham. It is reasonable to suppose that Thomas Thorpe might have used the first initials of Walsingham's name: "W" for Walsing, "H" for "Ham"—thus: "Mr. W.H."

Since, as I have hinted, Thorpe might well have had reason to obscure the Dedication, one of the ways he might have done so was to address Walsingham as "Mr."

This would presuppose that Thomas Thorpe—a St. Paul's Churchyard publisher—knew of Marlowe's authorship and of his association with Walsingham; and knew, further, of the entire imposture. I believe he did know, and that at least one other St. Paul's Churchyard publisher knew of the Shakespeare fraud.

So, laboriously, the pieces of the puzzle begin to fit.

12

AND with all this, what of Shakespeare? What of him as a person, as a literary force, as a professional during this period?

Nothing.

What of his colleagues? Did they comment upon this tight-lipped actor, who was certainly of their company? Not a word.

After William Shakespeare emerged, in his thirtieth year, and thereafter showered the stage with some of the most remarkable dramas in history, what comments did anyone make about him?

None.

How was Shakespeare (who never met Marlowe, directly or indirectly) affected by Marlowe's death, that Marlowe who was supposedly the strongest single "influence" on his professional work?

It was as though Marlowe had never lived.

Other dramatists lamented Marlowe's death. Why not Shakespeare? They were of the same age, both in their creative prime, both pursuing the same profession.

And again, when William Shakespeare died in 1616, who mourned him publicly in print, as was the custom following upon the deaths of all writers and dramatists of renown?

No one.

It was as though William Shakespeare had never lived or written.

13

AFTER *Venus and Adonis,* we next hear of Shakespeare in the title page of *The Rape of Lucrece,* printed in 1594. This poem was inspired by Marlowe's favorite poet, Ovid, whose works Marlowe had already translated while an undergraduate at Cambridge. Ovid, incidentally, recorded Lucretia's ravishment in his classic story, *Fasti,* which later became the plot of Shakespeare's poem, after Marlowe's assassination.

Following the publication of *Lucrece,* Shakespeare's name is next listed among performers acting at court—in December 1594. Then, five years after the Deptford tragedy—and only after five years—Shakespeare's name appears in the title page of *Love's Labour's Lost,* the first play that bore his name, although roughly sixteen plays had been written by 1598.

The fact that William Shakespeare's name was printed in the title page of an Elizabethan Quarto is, as we have seen, no surety of authorship. Eight of these Quarto dramas with the name William Shakespeare in their title pages had been rejected by reputable, conservative scholars and critics, as not Shakespeare's at all.

We know what the world thinks of William Shakespeare as a dramatist; an opinion based upon the thirty-six First Folio plays.

What does the world say of Marlowe, who before his so-called death had written only seven plays and a few poems? Herewith the critics on Marlowe:

Edward Phillips: "Christopher Marlowe, a kind of second Shakespeare."

Edmund Malone: "Christopher Marlowe was the most popular and admired dramatic poet of that age previous to the appearance of Shakespeare."

Charles Dilke: "Marlowe was the most famous poet of the [Elizabethan] age."

John Ingram: "To the date of his death, and, indeed, for some years after, Marlowe was evidently more esteemed as a poet, more beloved as a man, than ever Shakespeare himself."

J. O. Halliwell-Phillipps: "That Shakespeare commenced his literary vocation as a follower of Marlowe can hardly be denied."

A. W. Verity: "Marlowe created the noblest vehicle of dramatic expression of which any language is capable. He created a new dramatic form. He created in 'Edward II' a new type of play. . . . Shakespeare carried to its utmost limits . . . the dramas initiated by Marlowe. . . . In Shakespeare's 'Richard II' we have a continuation of the legitimate historical play first seen in Marlowe's 'Edward II.'"

R. L. Ashurst: "Marlowe was by far the greatest and strongest of Elizabethan dramatists; he had a powerful influence in the mental development of the poet we know as Shakespeare."

Sir Sidney Lee: "Marlowe alone . . . can be credited with exerting . . . a really substantial influence on Shakespeare."

Algernon Swinburne: "Marlowe is the greatest discoverer, the most daring and inspired pioneer, in all our poetic literature. Before Marlowe there was no genuine blank verse and genuine tragedy in our language. After his arrival the way was prepared, the path made straight, for Shakespeare."

William Allan Neilson: "Born in the same year as Shakespeare, Marlowe left behind him at 29 surpassing [dramatic] work. . . . In the vastness and intensity of his imagination, the splendid dignity of his verse, and the dazzling brilliance of his poetry, Marlowe exhibited the greatest genius that had appeared in the English drama."

Edward Dowden: "If Marlowe had lived longer and accomplished the work which lay clearly before him, he would have stood beside Shakespeare."

Robert M. Theobald: "Marlowe's tones are to be heard in even the most advanced of Shakespeare's plays. . . . There is an organic relation between Marlowe and Shakespeare which requires explanation. . . . There is an audacity about Shakespeare's diction which comes by direct descent from Marlowe."

Charles Grant: "Marlowe's 'Dr. Faustus' was the first work which bore the unmistakable impress of that tragic power which was to find its highest embodiment in 'King Lear,' 'Macbeth,' 'Hamlet' and 'Othello.' "

Thomas Marc Parrott: "Without Marlowe there would never have been the William Shakespeare whom we know."

Robert Adger Law: "No sufficient reason has yet been advanced for discarding the long accepted belief that Marlowe, at his death in 1593, was a dramatist and poet of far greater repute than was ever William Shakespeare."

J. M. Robertson: "Till long after his death, Marlowe held the stage in his own name with 'Dr. Faustus' and 'The Jew of Malta'; and under another's [Shakespeare's] name in 'Richard III.' . . . Marlowe was beloved for his circumnavigation of the soul. . . . If we are to know Marlowe, we must look through his eyes—the eyes of the most outstanding dramatist of the Elizabethan world before Shakespeare."

14

I HAVE earlier mentioned that my search began with my almost unconscious drawing of parallelisms between the works of Shakespeare and those of Marlowe.

Critics, of course, had long ago noted a resemblance between the works of these two writers. Ironically enough, it was in part this resemblance that gave rise to the praise of Marlowe's genius. But somehow this resemblance was never followed through to its surprising end.

Scholars have been content to assess the bond between the works of Marlowe and Shakespeare as a literary "influence." Going from the wealth of external evidence, which forced me to the conclusions I have detailed in this book, there is an even greater wealth of internal evidence to support my case.

When Thomas Marc Parrott—former professor of English at Princeton University, and expert in Elizabethan literature—remarked that "without Marlowe there never would have been the William Shakespeare whom we know" he was indulging in one of the literary understatements of the century. *Hamlet, King Lear,* any of the other dramatic masterpieces—had Marlowe never existed—would never have reached us in their present form.

Yet, is this not a strange admission?—that Shakespeare, a very great writer indeed, should have needed the literary back of Christopher Marlowe as a springboard to his own achievement? Perhaps influence is admissible in the case of lesser writers; though it is never too savory. But in the case of William Shakespeare it is lèse majesté indeed.

The nature of a literary influence, of a "style," in the works of two given authors must be expressed by a parallelism extracted therefrom.

The value of parallelisms is enormous. No one, with any authority, can lay claim to having deduced an "influence" in the stylistic relationship between two authors without offering parallelisms as evidence of that influence. A writer's literary style is as peculiarly his as his fingerprint. This, of course, is exceptionally true in writers of great genius. No one, for instance, who has read Bernard Shaw's *Saint Joan,* can ever again mistake the touch of the Sage of Ayot-St. Lawrence for the touch of any other playwright.

Sir Edmund K. Chambers was referring to this when he so aptly described the character of individuality in writing previously quoted in this book.

Oliver Elton, in his annual Shakespeare Lecture delivered to the British Academy in 1936, spoke of a writer's singleness of style :

> We must work . . . upward from the word and from the unit of rhythm; but also downward, starting from the conception, the character and the situation. Words and measures are, after all, only the artist's material; what is it that directs his choice and use of them?

The answer to this is as various, as complex, as simple, as the writer himself. Education, intelligence, attitudes, the palimpsest of a man's sensory and cerebral experience; all these determine his use and choice of words, if he is a writer; his brush strokes, his peculiar window on the world, if he is a painter—this is style.

All these things influence the artist. Parallelisms are merely a measuring stick, a rough one perhaps, but still as accurate as is humanly possible, by which we can try to grasp the mercury of a man's soul. Since we are certain of the similarity of style between Marlowe and Shakespeare—how many parallelisms, extracted from their plays and poems, constitute an "influence"? The best we can say is that a small number of parallelisms between any two authors denotes a valid influence of one author upon another; a tremendous number of them brands one of the authors as a plagiarist.

From the almost unlimited parallelisms that I have drawn from the works of Marlowe and Shakespeare, the verdict must be that the plays and poems of these two authors were written by the same person.

If Christopher Marlowe was actually murdered at the age of 29 and William Shakespeare did not commence to write until his thirtieth year, when did Marlowe's great influence take root? At once, is the reasonable answer. Yet this tremendous influence was generated by seven plays and a few poems written before Marlowe's death in 1593. And most of these efforts were not published until after 1593.

Where did William Shakespeare read these works of Marlowe's that influenced him so tremendously? Marlowe did not show his manuscripts to him. There is no evidence that the two men ever met; ever spoke to each other; ever referred to each other, directly or indirectly.

It is conceded that Shakespeare's period of productivity endured about twenty years, during which time he completed 36 plays, 154 sonnets, and two epic poems. Since we know that Marlowe's influence on the Bard did not cease until Shakespeare had written his last play (perhaps *The Tempest*), it is reasonable to wonder why one of the greatest poetic minds that ever lived permitted the influence of a lesser playwright throughout his creative life, even to the very end of it.

Surely William Shakespeare matures enough as a writer, over a twenty-year period, to develop his own style. Why should the ghost of another writer, whom he had never met,

124

continue to influence him in such extraordinary fashion? Why should Marlowe's earliest plays—among which *Tamburlaine* is perhaps the chief example—find echoes not alone in nearly all of Shakespeare's plays, but in practically all of the last plays that Shakespeare ever wrote? Plays like *King Lear, Macbeth,* and *Cymbeline*?

J. M. Robertson, a student of Elizabethan matters and a distinguished critic, was shocked at the thought that Shakespeare could be reduced to the level of an imitator of Marlowe. He compared Shakespeare's *Richard II* with Marlowe's *Edward II,* and was left stunned by their similarities. He stated that Shakespeare, on the strength of internal evidence, was nothing less than a "fumbling plagiarist" if his authorship of *Richard II* continued to be insisted on, as it still is, by scholars.

All this, despite the fact (of which Mr. Robertson must have been aware) that *Richard II* was written after Marlowe's 1593 death—so that to all intent and purpose—not to mention common sense—it would have been impossible for Marlowe to have written a word of the play; not from this side of the grave, anyhow.

Such anachronisms are anything but rare in Shakespearean study.

15

AT the back of this book, the reader will find a number of parallelisms, which, over the years, I have drawn from the works of Shakespeare and Marlowe. They comprise, by far, the largest number of Marlowe-Shakespeare parallelisms ever compiled.

All the parallelisms that I have gathered over the years are not given here. Their volume makes it impossible for them to be printed in a work of this kind; their number alone would require a separate volume.

With these parallelisms I hope to buttress my thesis. I believe that the discerning reader—and even the impatient one—will, after observing these similarities with even a casual eye, realize how apparent it is that one mind, one soul, conceived and gave birth to all the lines quoted.

Parallelisms, lifted from the work of two top dramatic poets and presented as evidence of a stylistic bond or influence, need not be identical in every letter, word, or syllable. When they are so alike, such examples would denote conscious plagiarism of one author from another.

This could, innocently enough, happen once or twice. Not protractedly.

The genuine artist and poet occasionally repeats himself verbatim. Significantly enough, the occasional verbatim parallelisms I quote from the works of Marlowe and Shakespeare reveal this striking tendency to self-repetition.

Only the third- or fourth-rate writer extendedly repeats the very letter and thought of another writer. Such geniuses as Marlowe and Shakespeare would never stoop to this.

In many instances, resemblance and repetition in the same author arise from the ability of a top literary mind to reshape and paraphrase, with infinite variation, a single thought.

Parallelisms, as I have said, need not be identical. They may be psychological, allusive, sentimental, topical. It is, however, unthinkable that William Shakespeare should repeat and duplicate whole words, whole phrases, whole sentences, whole thoughts, whole ideas, and even whole passages which first were found in the works of Christopher Marlowe.

And yet, that is precisely the case. The proof is in the back of this book; or in the works both of Marlowe and of Shakespeare.

There is only one reason for this literary twinning.

One mind conceived the plays and poems of William Shakespeare and those of Christopher Marlowe.

Before studying the larger number of parallelisms which are gathered in this volume, I list first, several parallelisms taken from the works of Shakespeare:

Titus Andronicus:
I'll dive into the burning lake below;

. . .

I am a mile beyond the moon.

Hamlet:
But I will delve one yard below their mines
And blow them at the moon.

Titus Andronicus:
He doth me wrong to feed me with delays.

Richard II:
He does me double wrong that wounds me with flatteries.

Romeo and Juliet (about Romeo of his dead Juliet):
He came with flowers to strew his lady's grave.

Hamlet (Hamlet to dead Ophelia):
I thought thy bride-bed to have decked, sweet maid
And not to have strewed thy grave.

Titus Andronicus:
Is not my sorrow deep, having no bottom?

Romeo and Juliet:
Is there no pity sitting in the clouds
That sees into the bottom of my grief?

Titus Andronicus:
When heaven doth weep, doth not the earth overflow?

Romeo and Juliet:
When the sun sets the air doth drizzle dew.

The Merchant of Venice:
I hold the world but a world,
A stage where every man must play his part
And mine a sad one.

As You Like It:
All the world's a stage and
All the men and women merely players.

Titus Andronicus:
This object kills me.

Othello:
The object poisons sight.

King Henry VI (Part II):
How irksome is this music to my heart!
When such strings jar, what hope of harmony?

Richard II:
. . . how sour sweet music is
When time is broke and no proportion kept.

Hamlet:
. . . let not ever
The soul of Nero enter this firm bosom.

The Merchant of Venice:
Let not the sound of shallow fopperies enter
My sober house.

Titus Andronicus:
'Twill vex thy soul.

King Lear:
Vex not his soul.

Hamlet:
This quarry cries havoc!

Julius Caesar:
. . . with a remorseless voice
Cries havoc.

Sonnet 29:
And trouble dead heaven with my bootless cries.

Titus Andronicus:
In bootless prayer have they been held up.

Titus Andronicus:
Romans, friends, followers,
Favourers of my right!

Julius Caesar:
Friends, Romans, Countrymen!

Titus Andronicus:
   That coddling spirit have they
   from their mother.

Julius Caesar:
   That rash humour which my
   mother gave me.

Titus Andronicus:
   She swooned almost at my pleas-
   ing tale.

Julius Caesar:
   Because Caesar refused the crown
   For he swooned and fell down.

King Lear:
   I have seen the day when with my
   good biting falchion
   I would have made them skip.

The Merry Wives of Windsor:
   I have seen the time with my long
   sword I would have made you
   four tall fellows skip like rats.

Othello:
   I have seen the day
   When with this little arm and
   with this good sword
   I have made my way through
   more impediments
   Than twenty times your stop.

Titus Andronicus:
   Witness these trenches made by
   grief and care.

Hamlet:
   Witness this army, or such mass
   and charge.

Titus Andronicus:
   My sons sweet blood will make it
   shame and blush.

Hamlet:
   O Shame, where is thy blush?

Titus Andronicus:
   To stir a mutiny in the mildest
   thought.

Julius Caesar:
   Let me not stir you up
   To such a sudden flood of mutiny.

There are thousands of these parallelisms in the works of Shakespeare and Marlowe. I ask the reader, who is the judge of my argument, to turn now to the back of this book and to study, as carefully as possible, the parallelisms quoted there. Such an interpretation is necessary, in order to follow properly the thread of my thesis as it continues to unroll.

The reader will find the study a curious one, and not without its excitement.

Having studied these parallelisms, the mind behind them is unmasked.

It is impossible for a man of Shakespeare's caliber to have so slavishly imitated and repeated another writer throughout the whole of his creative life. To believe that Shakespeare is the author of the Canon ascribed to him is also to believe that he is one of the greatest literary thieves of all time.

J. M. Robertston draws another conclusion:

> Such absolute duplication of another man's ideas [i.e., on the basis of *Richard II*] would prove, if anything, that Shakespeare felt himself unequal to the invention of new ones.

This, then, is the William Shakespeare of *Richard II*.

This is the William Shakespeare whose name appeared on eight plays rejected as spurious by conservative Shakespearean scholars.

This is the William Shakespeare whose first work, *Venus and Adonis,* appeared four months after Christopher Marlowe's legal death, with Shakespeare in his thirtieth year, already in Elizabethan middle age.

This is the William Shakespeare who wrote *Pericles*. This play is an orphan of the Shakespeare Canon. It was denied Shakespeare's paternity by John Heming and Henry Condell when they christened the First Folio of 1623. Very simply, they did not include *Pericles*.

Pericles was printed for the first time, in quarto form, in 1609, and had been registered with the Stationers Company by Edward Blount a year before, in 1608—the same Blount who had published Marlowe's *Hero and Leander* in 1598— the same Blount who was the "prime mover" in bringing out the Shakespeare First Folio of 1623.

And yet, with marvelous inconsistency, *Pericles* for the past two hundred years has been accepted by almost every single scholar of note as a product of William Shakespeare's brain. *Pericles* has appeared in practically every edition of the plays for more than two centuries.

This has been condoned on the grounds of a recognizable style—internal evidence; a style that must be compared, naturally, to that of the First Folio plays.

A study in illogic.

16

A WRITER'S style is not a rigid thing. It changes, grows, with the man. As he matures, so can his style. It is interesting to see the geometric progression of style in "Shakespeare's" plays, as he proceeds from his earliest works to his latest; from, for example, *Love's Labour's Lost, The Comedy of Errors, King John,* and the three parts of *Henry VI,* as his earlier plays, to *Henry VIII, Cymbeline, Measure for Measure,* and *The Tempest,* as some of his later ones.

Then, if you will, study the progression of style in Marlowe's works—from *Tamburlaine* to *Edward II.* Chart this growth, and you will find, as have many Shakespearean critics, that Marlowe's earliest plays contain within themselves the elements that come to their fulfillment in the latest dramas of William Shakespeare.

Which is why orthodox scholars—even though they accept the story of Marlowe's assassination—cannot help seeing Marlowe's hand in a number of Shakespearean plays. As usual, we are again faced with the illogic of the literary conservative, who must take on faith a situation he cannot rationalize.

Some scholars, under the authority of the rule of style, assign a number of the canonical Shakespearean dramas, in whole or in part, to the hand of Christopher Marlowe— Marlowe who lay buried in the parish churchyard at Deptford when these plays were written.

Again, logical illogic. Herewith some of the plays assigned to Marlowe by orthodox scholarship, with commentary:

Titus Andronicus

Edmund Malone: "Written by Christopher Marlowe."

Herman Ulrici: ". . . exhibits a resemblance to the style of Marlowe."

A. W. Verity: ". . . in great part the work of Marlowe."

Gerald Massey: ". . . mapped out and partly written by Marlowe."

James Boswell: "Much more in the style of Marlowe."

William Hazlitt: "Marlowe has a much fairer claim to be the author of 'Titus Andronicus' than Shakespeare . . . from internal evidence."

Georg Brandes: "Certain peculiar turns of phrase in 'Titus Andronicus' remind us . . . of Marlowe."

F. G. Fleay: Attributes *Titus Andronicus* to Marlowe.

Richard III

Jane Lee: " 'Richard III' is full of . . . Marlowe's soul and spirit."

F. E. Schelling: "Some assign a hand n 'Richard III' to Christopher Marlowe; others regard it as a joint production of Marlowe and Shakespeare. . . . 'Richard III' shows the influence of Marlowe to a greater degree than any play of Shakespeare's."

S. S. Ashbaugh: "There is far more of Marlowe than of Shakespeare in 'Richard III.' "

A. W. Pollard: "There is no room for both Shakespeare and Marlowe in the play."

Edward Dowden: "A certain resemblance . . . to the ideal manner of Marlowe."

Sir Israel Gollancz: "Richard like [Marlowe's] Tamburlaine [in *Tamburlaine*] or Faustus [in *Dr. Faustus*] or Barabas [in

The Jew of Malta] monopolizes the whole action of the drama."

F. G. Fleay: " 'Richard III' bears strong internal evidence of Marlowe's craftsmanship . . ."

Sir Sidney Lee: "Throughout 'Richard III' Shakespeare's effort to emulate Marlowe is undeniable."

A. W. Verity:" 'Richard III' approximates the peculiar type of drama represented by Marlowe's 'Tamburlaine,' 'Jew of Malta' and 'Dr. Faustus.' "

Julius Caesar

Among scholars who give *Julius Caesar* to Christopher Marlowe—from a major to a minor share—are E. H. C. Oliphant, William Wells, and J. M. Robertson.

Richard II

There is near consensus by critics that the "influence" of Marlowe is omnipresent in *Richard II*—that the whole play originated from Marlowe's *Edward II*. A few have articulated this "influence":

William Allan Neilson: "The subject of 'Richard II' may have been suggested by Marlowe's 'Edward II.' "

Sir Sidney Lee: "Shakespeare plainly disclosed a conscious . . . resolve to follow in . . . Marlowe's footsteps. . . . 'Richard II' was clearly suggested by Marlowe's 'Edward II.' "

F. E. Schelling: "In 'Richard II' Shakespeare still had . . . Marlowe in view."

Priscilla Fletcher: " 'Richard II' is modeled certainly upon Marlowe."

A. W. Verity: " 'Richard II' was written on a model furnished by Marlowe."

Henry VI (Parts I, II, III)

Some critics give Marlowe the authorship of these three historical plays outright. Numerous students assign a major portion of them to Marlowe. A great number acknowledge at least some part of Marlowe in each of the plays. Among those who comment upon the trilogy, suggesting Marlowe as the author of either one, or all, of the plays, are: A. W. Verity, Felix Schelling, Edmund Malone, Richard Farmer, George Chalmers.

Other critics have commented as follows:

Algernon Swinburne: "Marlowe was more or less concerned in the production . . . of these plays."

Jane Lee: "Marlowe may have collaborated with Shakespeare."

C. F. Tucker Brooke: "Marlowe, the only Elizabethan writer who, in my opinion, has any demonstrable interest in these plays."

Alexander Dyce: "There is a strong suspicion that . . . the plays are wholly by Marlowe."

Ashley H. Thorndike: "Marlowe's influence, if not his hand, is dominant."

Other scholars have detected Marlowe's influence in one or all of the three plays, which first saw the light of day in the First Folio of 1623—although Parts II and III were published anonymously under other titles, in 1595.

John Bakeless, biographer and Elizabethan researcher, whose attitude is that of a self-confessed Shakespearean conservative, concludes that "the influence of Marlowe appears to be important" in the following plays of Shakespeare:

> The Merchant of Venice
> Henry VI, Part I
> Henry VI, Part II
> Henry VI, Part III
> Julius Caesar
> Richard III
> Titus Andronicus
> Richard II

The Taming of a Shrew (source play
for "The Taming of the Shrew")

Bakeless further states that "there are faint traces of Marlowe" in the following plays and poems accredited to Shakespeare:

Romeo and Juliet	Henry IV
Venus and Adonis	A Midsummer Night's Dream
King Lear	Hamlet
Much Ado About Nothing	Sonnets
King John	Rape of Lucrece
The Merry Wives of Windsor	Troilus and Cressida
As You Like It	Antony and Cleopatra

Bakeless comments: "The exact relationship of these two major figures is the chiefest puzzle of literary history."

Another Shakespearean conservative, who has defended the authenticity of the Canon in numerous articles, books, and monographs, is J. M. Robertson, who, before his death, was a member of Parliament and an outspoken Shakespearean scholar. Mr. Robertson stated that Christopher Marlowe, on the basis of verse tests, must have had a hand in the following First Folio plays:

The Comedy of Errors	Richard II
The Merchant of Venice	King Henry VI, Part I
Titus Andronicus	King Henry VI, Part II
Hamlet	King Henry VI, Part III
The Taming of the Shrew	Henry V
Richard III	Romeo and Juliet
Julius Caesar	Macbeth

Here, then, is the amusing, if ironic, spectacle of conservative Shakespearean scholarship, orthodox to the last, confirming Marlowe's authorship, sole or in part, in more than half the works of William Shakespeare, most of which were written after Marlowe's "murder."

It is fair to say that William Shakespeare's authenticity as author of the works ascribed to him is in part damned by the very men who defend him.

There is only one way of slashing through this hedgerow of contradictions. Christopher Marlowe was not murdered at Deptford. Else, how could his hand be detected in the creation of works not yet written at the time of his death?

But there is further proof for my thesis. Let us turn to Dr. Thomas Corwin Mendenhall, professor at the college that later became Ohio State University, who revealed more than fifty years ago that he had developed a plan of investigation whereby the identity of an author, through his writing, could scientifically be detected—that, from a mechanical point of view, a style of composition would be uniquely individual throughout:

> Nearly twenty years ago [i.e., about 1880] I devised a method for exhibiting graphically such peculiarities of style in literary composition as seemed to be almost purely mechanical, and of which an author would be absolutely unconscious.
>
> The chief merit of the method consisted in the fact that its application required no experience of judgment—accurate enumeration being all that was necessary. By displaying one or more phases of the mechanism of composition, characteristics might be revealed which the author could make no attempt to conceal, being himself unaware of their existence.
>
> It was further assumed that owing to the well-known persistence of unconscious habit, personal peculiarities in the construction of sentences, in use of either short or long words, in the number of words in a sentence, etc., would, in the long run, manifest themselves with such regularity that their graphic representations would become a means of identification.

Dr. Mendenhall undertook to experiment with the works of twenty noted poets and prose writers. The guinea pigs included such distinguished figures as Percy Shelley, John Keats, Sir Walter Scott, William Thackeray, John Stuart Mill, Lord Byron.

The investigator set himself to the Herculean task of

counting each letter of every word in the representative works of each writer being tested.

He set up graphs of the characteristic curve of each model author which would reflect a predisposition to use a vocabulary containing anywhere from one- to fifteen-letter words. These graphs, when compared, revealed the fact that each author possessed his own characteristic peculiarities in the use of certain lettered words.

The tests were then computed mathematically, down to the minutest decimal.

No two were alike.

The conclusion, therefore, was that no two authors will, mechanically, write identically.

Dr. Mendenhall then laid aside his work. He had proved his theory.

Toward the end of the century, Dr. Mendenhall received an urgent communication from a wealthy Shakespeare enthusiast requesting an appointment. After the meeting in Boston, Dr. Mendenhall was assigned a tremendous task.

The wealthy Bostonian, he was informed, was a champion of Francis Bacon as the author of Shakespeare's plays and poems. Hearing of Dr. Mendenhall's study, the Baconian wished to retain him to test his theory through the mechanical, graphological method, to prove that Lord Bacon actually wrote the Works of Shakespeare.

Several women were hired for research. Their task was to assemble the works of various authors, and count the letters of more than two million words dredged from the works of Ben Jonson, Oliver Goldsmith, Francis Beaumont, John Fletcher, Christopher Marlowe, Lord Lytton, William Shakespeare, Joseph Addison, and a group of several then-modern authors, as controls.

After many months (the women would work only from three to five hours a day—had they sustained the count longer they would have been left in a state of collapse) the letters of more than two million words had been counted and tabulated: 200,000 from Bacon, from his *Advancement of Learning*, the prose history of his *Henry VIII*, and a number of shorter essays; 75,000 from the plays of Ben Jonson; all the words from the seven plays of Christopher Marlowe; 400,000 from the Works of William Shakespeare; and well over a million words from the numerous other authors examined.

Dr. Mendenhall began to make graphs for each writer under analysis, and then computed the individual reckonings on a percentage basis. The wealthy Baconian waited tensely for his expensive answer.

Dr. Mendenhall started to plot the characteristic curves of Bacon and Shakespeare onto each other's finished charts. He didn't have to finish the job. A single glance ruled out any possibility of similitude.

Shakespeare's vocabulary, the diagram revealed, consisted of words averaging four letters in length. The words used with the greatest frequency also were four-letter words. This was, as Dr. Mendenhall told his employer, "a thing never met with before" in the works of any other writer he had analyzed.

Bacon's graph, on the other hand, showed constant use of much longer words. The graphs of other writers were entirely different from one another. From Jonson to Beaumont to Addison to Lord Lytton—each writer disclosed his own peculiarity of style in composition.

And then the professor diagnosed Christopher Marlowe's works. This is what he had to say:

> It was in the counting and plotting of the plays of Christopher Marlowe, however, that something akin to a sensation was produced among those actually engaged in the work. In the characteristic curve of his plays Christopher Marlowe agrees with Shakespeare as well as Shakespeare agrees with himself.

The printed transcripts of these tests are available. It is incredible to observe how absolutely identical are the characteristic curves of these so-called "different" authors.

And on this note Dr. Mendenhall ends his study.

He had wrought better than he knew. As far as he was concerned, Marlowe had been killed in a tavern brawl (remember, all this happened in 1902) in 1593. He could not possibly have written Shakespeare's plays. The study receded into oblivion, from whence I have carefully exhumed it, to present it here as only one of the supporting foundations for my argument.

17

AS each facet of the truth of Marlowe authorship is bur-
nished by research, Marlowe's own reaction to the imposture that he so unwillingly shared is of interest.

Certainly, if my argument is sound, Marlowe must have
been one of the most tortured men in history. We have already seen evidence of his unhappiness in the *Sonnets*. But
what of his plays? It is probable that Marlowe, the perpetual
exile, an exile even in his own country, would not have
resisted the desire to allude, in whatever indirect fashion, to
his unique and miserable fate. He must have been tempted
to refer to the twists of his ironic destiny. And if so, did he
succumb to the temptation, and hide the truth behind the
poetry of the plays that we know as William Shakespeare's?

I believe that he did. In fact, I feel certain of it.

In one play alone (a play written after Marlowe had completed the English history cycle, and had not yet created
Lear, Timon, and *The Tempest*—a play written at least seven
years after the conspiracy) Marlowe did indeed refer to his
position, mocking the world with a bitter glee. He dared
not specifically mention the fraud in which he, Walsingham,
and his publisher-acquaintances had all conspired to keep
alive. Heads would have rolled immediately had he done so,
and his life would have been forfeit for the second time;
and this time he would not have come back from the grave.

But before proceeding to his amazing play, let us look for

a moment at *The Jew of Malta,* in which a wholly astonishing reference by Marlowe himself as having been alive after 1593 seems to have been made.

So far as we know, the earliest mention of *The Jew of Malta* was February 26, 1592, when it was first produced in a London theater. The play belonged apparently to Philip Henslowe, theatrical broker, who listed it in his *Diary* as having been presented on various stages between 1592 and 1596. During those years *The Jew of Malta* was played no less than thirty-six times—a genuine hit by Elizabethan standards. It was one of the most popular stage plays of the time.

Marlowe's *The Jew of Malta* was registered with the Stationers Company on May 17, 1594, by Thomas Millington and Nicholas Linge—the latter was to publish the authentic Quarto of Shakespeare's *Hamlet* in 1604. The earliest published version of *The Jew of Malta,* however, is the Quarto of 1633, which, incidentally, attests that it was "written by Christopher Marlo." The 1633 published Quarto appears to be the only edition of the drama ever printed, as far as we know.

No one knows why the play was first published almost forty years after it had been registered and ready for the press. We know not why its printing was halted and its text not made available until as much as four decades later.

What is significant about the play is that the character who speaks the Prologue—Machevil—and who does not appear again in the drama recites some three dozen lines which are a remarkable confirmation of the myth of Marlowe's 1593 "murder."

Since *The Jew of Malta* is an acknowledged play of Christopher Marlowe's, it must of necessity have been written before 1593. But was the Prologue written before or after 1593? Professor C. F. Tucker Brooke, an orthodox Elizabethan authority, tells us: "It is quite true, as Wagner has argued, that this Prologue of Machevil may possibly have been written after the play."

If we accept Tucker Brooke's reasoning, it then becomes possible, in the light of my argument, for Marlowe to have written the Prologue after his own faked death.

Before quoting the lines referred to above, let us refer back to Robert Greene's *Groatsworth of Wit*. In one of the many mournful bits of advice proffered in that famous pamphlet, Greene asks Marlowe, "Is it pestilent Machevilian policy thou hast studied?" Since Greene identified Marlowe in this fashion, it is not inconceivable that our poet might have been known under the nickname of Machevil—the unscrupulous Florentine. In fact, from our knowledge of Christopher Marlowe's character, it is more than just conceivable. I have never held brief for him as a saintly character.

It is not implausible, therefore, that years later, in writing the Prologue to his completed play, *The Jew of Malta*, Marlowe might have been the very character—in flesh as well as fancy—who spoke the Prologue.

Here is a partial explanation for the forty-year lag between the registering of the play and its publication. The incriminating nature of the Prologue might well have played a part in forcing a long time gap before the printing of *The Jew of Malta*.

Here are the lines:

Albeit the world think Machevil is dead,
Yet was his soul but flown beyond the Alps,
And now the Guize is dead, is come from France
To view this land [i.e., Britain] and frolic with his friends.
To some, perhaps my name is odious,
But such as love me guard me from their tongues,
And let them know that I am Machevil,
And weigh not men, and therefore not men's words:
Admired I am of those that hate me most.
Though some speak openly against my books
Yet will they read me, and thereby attain

To Peter's chair.

But .   .   .   .   I come not, I
To read a lecture here in Britain.

Let me take the liberty, now, of paraphrasing the context of the lines just quoted. Observe the pattern of the Marlowe-Shakespeare imposture, as it is revealed in the Prologue to Marlowe's play:

> Although the world thinks, I, Marlowe, have died,
> Yet I—my soul—had fled beyond the Alps, to Italy,
> And now the Guize [symbolic reference to a high government authority in England, who, being alive, prevented my return] is dead,
> I, Marlowe, can now come from France [to which country I traveled from Italy]
> To view my beloved England and visit, once again, my friends —Walsingham, Blount and Thorpe, for example.
> To some perhaps—my known enemies—the name Marlowe is odious;
> But such as love me [and know of my being alive] guard [my name] from their tongues,
> And let them—my enemies—know I am not Marlowe, but someone else [Machevil, or, say, another name].
> I, Marlowe, weigh not men—the multitudes—nor their words —and therefore do not care what the vulgar think.
> I am admired [i.e., my creative superiority is both admired and envied] of those who hate me most;
> Though some people will and have spoken openly against my writings because of my horrible reputation,
> Yet will they read my books—my poems and dramas—charmed by my ability to attain—as they in turn attain—the highest heaven of beauty's perfection.
> But I have not returned to Britain to read you a lecture on my "rebirth"!

Meditate on this, please. It is not wishful thinking.

And now we come to the pastoral comedy *As You Like It,* which was included in the First Folio of 1623 as one of the thirty-six dramas ascribed to William Shakespeare.

In no other single piece of the collected Works has reference been so bluntly made by Marlowe to his authorship not only of *As You Like It,* but of every play in the Canon.

The role played by the character Touchstone—the Clown—is one of the pivotal parts in the secondary theme of the play.

Significantly enough, this character was not christened with the name Touchstone by the author in the 1623 First Folio version—the authentic version of the drama. In the First Folio the author identified every word of dialogue spoken by this character with the name "Clown." Apparently, it was only after the play was completed—as a sudden afterthought—that it was decided to call the clown Touchstone.

Throughout the whole First Folio version of the play the name Touchstone is officially recognized but once—in the listing of three characters as they make their entrance, Act II, Scene IV. Identification is made in this unusual fashion: "Clown, alias Touchstone." As the story progresses, the sobriquet appears but twice in passing.

Were it not for the authentic, First Folio *As You Like It,* the character of Touchstone would never have appeared as such. His part would simply have been named "Clown."

Normally, this peculiar name switch would not be important. But in the light of what Touchstone has to say in the play, the name change becomes significant indeed. I find no other alternative but to conclude that the author (or some other person), knowing what the name "Touchstone" really meant, caused it to be placed alongside the character "Clown" as "Clown, alias Touchstone."

There was a reason for this—a special reason.

Touchstone is not known to be either a Christian name or a surname. A touchstone is a black stone which, while not precious in itself, reveals preciousness in whatever it touches.

The person who had the name, Touchstone, inserted into the listing of the characters in Act II, Scene IV, knew the meaning of the word. The Clown's words, in touching upon the secret (that Marlowe was responsible for the play), would reveal the preciousness of that secret. Hence, a touchstone.

In Act III, Scene III, of *As You Like It,* Touchstone addresses the rustic damsel Audrey:

> I am here with thee and thy goats, as the most capricious poet, honest Ovid, was among the Goths.

Placed in the texture of a delicately conceived, Elizabethan pastoral, what do these words mean? Are they just banter, as they seem?

I do not believe so. In the first place, the words are not banter; in the second place, they certainly do not apply to Audrey; in the third place, they have not been analyzed in relation to the two characters throughout the centuries of criticism.

We know that Ovid was one of Christopher Marlowe's great literary influences.

We know, historically, that Ovid, like Marlowe, suffered banishment from his native land for professing certain ideas which incurred the wrath of authority. Ovid was banished to the land of the Goths—Marlowe was enduring, perhaps at the very moment he was writing *As You Like It,* banishment from his native England, to another pastoral country.

The comparison that Marlowe made of his own fate with that of Ovid is both gleeful and ironical.

Touchstone's seeming banter with Audrey is in reality an exposition of Marlowe's own fate for those who have eyes to see and ears to hear.

Let me paraphrase slightly:

> I am here with thee and thy goats, as the most capricious poet, honest Ovid, was among the Goths

becomes:

> I, Marlowe, am banished to this goatish, wild, yet pastoral country just as, strangely enough, my idol, the whimsical and

capricious poet, honest Ovid, was banished to the Barbarous Goths.

The next words that the Clown—or Touchstone—utters to Audrey are these:

> When a man's verses cannot be understood, nor a man's good wit seconded with the forward child, Understanding, it strikes a man more dead than a great reckoning in a little room.

When Audrey answers that she does not know what he is talking about, Touchstone replies:

> . . . the truest poetry is the most feigning.

Now, Audrey has a point. In truth, taken in literal context, no one, including Audrey, can possibly know what Touchstone is talking about. There is no reason for him to speak these lines. There is no motivation in them. The entire speech is highly irrelevant to the play.

These lines were obviously inserted because the author had a motive for writing them. They were placed there with deliberate purpose.

My verses, Marlowe is telling us, "cannot be understood." And this irony strikes him more cruelly than the official cause of his death:

> . . . it strikes a man more dead than a great reckoning in a little room.

But how did Marlowe know of the official cause of his death? Earlier in this book I suggested that the poet and Sir Thomas Walsingham might have collaborated in searching out a reason for the contrived murder; that a quarrel over a reckoning would be a common enough grievance, and a good enough reason for a fatal brawl. Since Marlowe was privy to the murder of May 30, 1593, it becomes clear how the author of *As You Like It* was able to quote the exact "cause" of Marlowe's own death.

Would William Shakespeare—had he written the play—

have been privy to the exact circumstances of Marlowe's "assassination"? Would he have known of the "great reckoning in a little room"?

How? Remember, there is no evidence that Shakespeare and Marlowe ever knew or were interested one in the other.

Since Danby's Report had been quietly laid away in the files of the Public Record Office for 332 years—how could William Shakespeare have gained access to it? It has been seen that none of Marlowe's contemporaries knew anything of the real facts behind Marlowe's murder; for several years after his death they believed that he died of the then raging plague. It would have been impossible for William Shakespeare to gain knowledge of this beautifully kept secret.

Again, the odd phrase that comes at the end of "it strikes a man more dead than a great reckoning in a little room" is a curious echo of Marlowe's own phraseology. In his play *The Jew of Malta,* Barabas speaks the line: "Infinite riches in a little room"—another of the parallelisms that abound so strangely in the works of Marlowe and Shakespeare.

Now, out of the nearly one thousand characters that populate Shakespeare's plays—running the gamut from kings to clowns—there is only one character out of the enormous total called William—just unadorned "William." William appears in Act V, Scene I, of *As You Like It*—and takes on tremendous significance.

William is an ignorant, uneducated rustic. In one of the shortest scenes in the play, the only one in which he appears, William is the target and protagonist for Touchstone. As Touchstone's inarticulate and stupid rival, he is ridiculed by the latter for his ignorance. Touchstone hurls this scornful censure into William's teeth:

> For all your writers do consent that ipse is he; now, you are not ipse, for I am he.

What sense does all this make? There is no reason buried

148

in the motivation of the play that warrants this abstruse banter. In the light of the imposture, however, it takes on frightening significance.

Ipse, of course, is the Latin approximation for "I myself." Paraphrased, Touchstone's diatribe against William reads:

> For all your perceptive writers, and readers, agree and consent that ipse—I myself—am the author; now you, William Shakespeare, are not ipse—I myself—for I, Marlowe, am he—the author.

And, again, herewith the lines that just precede those quoted. They also are addressed to William and form part of the preface to the "ipse" lines:

> . . . for it is a figure in rhetoric that drink, being poured out of a cup into a glass, by filling the one doth empty the other; for all your writers do consent that ipse is he . . .

Once more, what does all this mean? Unless interpreted in the light of the imposture, the words have not the barest justification; they should never have been written. What it can only mean is that Marlowe had emptied his cup of authorship into the glass of William's (Shakespeare's) pseudo authorship. Thus, by filling the one (Shakespeare) it "doth empty the other" (Marlowe).

Also observe that the author, in Act IV, Scene I, saw fit to speak knowingly of Hero and Leander. Few, if any, Elizabethan dramatists were so enamored of these two mythological figures as Christopher Marlowe. In many of his plays Marlowe speaks of his affection for these legendary lovers.

He also wrote a poem about them—the exquisite *Hero and Leander*.

In three additional plays, the author of the First Folio refers to *Hero and Leander*; again, in *The Two Gentlemen of Verona, A Midsummer Night's Dream,* and *Much Ado About Nothing*. It would make the strongest sort of sense to believe that Marlowe pursues the love-myth so close to his 'heart in the other plays that, according to this argument, he wrote.

On the other hand, there is no evidence that Shakespeare was interested or had any knowledge of these two mythological characters. Why should he, for no dramaturgical reason, refer to these characters, as he does, in so many of his dramas? There is no reason to be found.

The reference to Hero and Leander in *As You Like It,* as well as in the other plays in which this couple is mentioned, is a typical Marlovian touch.

We come now to a quotation from Act III, Scene V, of the play:

> Dead shepherd! now I find thy saw of might,
> "Who ever loved that loved not at first sight?"

Perhaps more than any other two lines in the Canon, this couplet has been the cause of misconception and delusion.

The historic misinterpretation given these lines is almost of the same magnitude as Robert Greene's allusion to a "shake-scene" in his *Groatsworth of Wit*—with which we have previously dealt. Sir Sidney Lee started the misconception of the couplet, which students of the Elizabethan drama have paid homage to for many generations:

In *As You Like It,* generations of scholars inform us, Shakespeare parenthetically commemorates his acquaintance with Marlowe by apostrophizing him in the lines:

> Dead shepherd! now I find thy saw of might,
> "Who ever loved that loved not at first sight?"

Since there is, as I have repeatedly stated, throughout this book not a grain of evidence that William Shakespeare and Christopher Marlowe ever met, knew each other, or spoke, or read anything to or about each other, this statement is suspect from the start. Conjecture and wishful thinking perhaps; but fact, no.

The second line of this couplet is nothing less than a quotation from Christopher Marlowe's own work. You will find it in Marlowe's poem, *Hero and Leander*. Obviously, Shakespeare duplicated it, word for word.

But why? And how do the scholars reach the interpretation that the couplet is a commemoration of Christopher Marlowe?

This is the genesis of their reasoning: The words "dead shepherd" represent Shakespeare's suddenly tender remembrance of Marlowe, of whose death at Deptford he was aware. Caught up in this recollection, he recalls his friend's gentleness and, after addressing him as "dead shepherd," quotes the line from his dead friend's poem, *Hero and Leander*, a line which he especially cherished.

But there is no testimony—not one whit—to support this reasoning. The interpretation can be seen only as unmitigated wishful thinking.

And even if for purposes of argument we concede that the couplet does refer to Marlowe—why should Shakespeare remember his "friend" (whom he had never met or spoken to) so touchingly in this couplet when, a few moments before, he deliberately had mocked his "friend's" death and murder thus:

> When a man's verses cannot be understood . . . it strikes a man more dead than a great reckoning in a little room.

First, Shakespeare mocks his friend cruelly; then, a few pages farther on, he remembers him with tenderness and reverence.

Now, if we assume that Christopher Marlowe wrote *As You Like It*, what is the origin of the couplet and to whom did he allude? It is apparent that he referred to someone. I believe it to be Sir Philip Sidney.

Let us for the moment return to Marlowe's patron. Sir Thomas Walsingham was second cousin, as we know, to Sir Francis Walsingham, Queen Elizabeth's Secretary of State.

The two Walsinghams were on the closest of terms. From documents we find that Sir Francis' daughter married Sir Philip Sidney. The original marriage contract can still be viewed in Sidney's castle, Penshurst, not far from Canterbury, Marlowe's birthplace; and closer still to Scadbury Park, Chislehurst, Walsingham's estate.

We know that Sir Thomas was fascinated by poetry in general and poets in particular. There is little doubt that, as Marlowe's patron, he spoke about Sir Philip Sidney, whom he certainly knew; and discussed, with Marlowe, Sidney's poetry.

Marlowe's especial interest in Sidney is, therefore, easily established.

Sir Philip was killed on the battlefield of Flanders in 1586. He was Marlowe's senior by ten years, and when he died he was 32 years old. Marlowe was 22 at the time, still a student at Cambridge University. (Of Shakespeare, of course, we know nothing.) Sidney had written a number of poems all of which were published after his death. We are concerned here, however, with one only—*Astrophel and Stella*—a collection of sonnets—which first appeared in print in 1591 and which was, as Sir Sidney Lee remarked, the sole cause

> . . . that the sonnet enjoyed . . . any conspicuous and continuous favor.

Marlowe must have read and known *Astrophel and Stella*. Lee observed:

> Sidney enjoyed in the decade that followed his death the reputation of a demi-god, and the wide dissemination in print of his numerous sonnets in 1591 spurred nearly every living poet in England to emulate his achievement.

It is certain, therefore, that Christopher Marlowe was familiar with Sidney's *Astrophel*. To bolster this statement, I quote below eight lines from a sonnet in *Astrophel and Stella* which trace to their source the origin of the famous couplet, which supposedly marked Shakespeare's reference to Marlowe's memory:

> Not at first sight, nor with a dribbled shot
> Love gave the wound, which while I breathe will bleed;
> But known worth did in time of mine proceed,
> Till by degrees it had full conquest got;
> I saw and liked, I liked but loved not.
> I loved, but straight did not what love decreed,
> At length to love's decree I, forced, agreed,
> Yet with repining at so partial lot.

These lines are surely the chrysalis from which Marlowe's own line

> who ever loved that loved not at first sight

budded.

It is certainly more than possible that the lines paraphrased from Sidney's *Astrophel and Stella,* which began with the tag "dead shepherd," made reference to Sir Philip Sidney, the adored dead poet.

And so another link in the chain of evidence is forged.

18

THERE is in *As You Like It* a character extraneous to the plot. The scene in which this character appears is supernumerary and could be excised without for a moment disturbing the continuity of the drama.

His name is Sir Oliver Martext. He is wantonly, almost clumsily, introduced into the play; this by an author who is known for many things, but not for clumsiness in character introduction. Yet, there must be a purpose for Martext.

The significance of the character lies only in his name. Oliver is a proper Christian name, certainly; Martext, of course, is obviously synthetic.

What was the author's intent? What was his reason, his compelling reason for introducing an unnecessary character? *As You Like It* provides the reason; it is, of course, the touchstone to the problem of authorship; it is the only play out of the thirty-six in the Folio in which Marlowe dared hint at his identity.

Martext has come down the centuries as one continuous proper name. Every edition has printed the surname unhyphened. But the First Folio version of *As You Like It*, printed unquestionably from the original author's manuscript, clearly hyphens the character's name, as Mar-text—the only character so hyphened out of the more than twenty in the play.

Mar-text, or, more properly, Marlowe's-text, is the way

that Christopher Marlowe chose to reveal the secret of his authorship.

Roundabout? Certainly. But please remember that every time Marlowe punned or joked about his identity he risked the headsman's ax, not only for himself but for the few people involved in the great deception. Only in the most roundabout way could he refer to the imposture.

Further, only three short sentences in all are spoken by Mar-text. His unimportance in the play is emphasized by the meagerness of his role. The purpose of the character could only be to hint that Marlowe was still around, amused but desperate, and always indulging in a dour allusion to his afterlife.

To crown the self-confession, there are Mar-text's final words, as if a valedictory:

> . . . ne'er a fantastical knave of them all shall flout me out of my calling.

Marlowe was amusing himself—and coming perilously close to revealing the fact that he was alive—and that the Queen's justice had been thoroughly tricked and set at naught.

His friends' lives were certainly at stake. It was fortunate that someone privy to the imposture, probably one of Marlowe's friends (it could, at a guess, have been Walsingham or Edward Blount), read the manuscript and recognized the danger it concealed before it was published. And, in the nick of time, prevented it from being published. There is documentary evidence for this.

As You Like It was registered August 4, 1600, with the Stationers Company, a customary prelude to publication. For no reason, and quite suddenly, a caveat was placed upon the play, and duly set down in the books of the Stationers Company:

> A book to be stayed.

And stayed it was. For twenty-three years *As You Like It* was neither published nor produced in London theaters, or anywhere else. It first saw the light of day in the First Folio of 1623. It was the only drama of the thirty-six in the Folio ever to be so entered in the Register, and then be published in 1623.

Someone had recognized the danger and acted promptly, with a sure and crushing hand.

19

ALTHOUGH Marlowe's *Hero and Leander* was registered with the Stationers Company on September 28,
1593, it was not published until five years later—in 1598—
by Edward Blount. The poem carried Marlowe's name in the
title page, and contained in two "sestiads," or parts, the tale
of the mythological lovers. A subsequent printing of *Hero
and Leander,* which was, queerly enough, brought out the
same year (1598), contained the completed version of the
poem—four additional sestiads, which brought the number
of parts to six. The title page of the fuller edition states that
it was

> Begun by Christopher Marlowe;
> and finished by George Chapman.

Marlowe's name, however, is printed in the title page in
larger and bolder type than Chapman's.

The conclusion of Elizabethan scholars, naturally enough,
is that the poem, left unfinished by Christopher Marlowe at
the time of his reported 1593 murder, was completed by
George Chapman.

It is worth noting that a subsequent edition of *Hero and
Leander,* brought out in 1600, though it contained both
finished and unfinished versions, did not ascribe to George
Chapman his previous share in the poem. This same 1600
edition, though it advertised the presence of Christopher

Marlowe's translation of the *First Book of Lucan,* for some inexplicable reason failed to carry the translation at all.

Meanwhile, for the record, here is the Dedication of *Hero and Leander* addressed to Marlowe's patron by the publisher Edward Blount:

> To the Right Worshipful,
> Sir Thomas Walsingham, Knight.
> Sir:
> We think not ourselves discharged of the duty we owe to our friend [i.e., Christopher Marlowe] when we have brought the breathless body to the earth:
> For albeit the eye there taketh his ever farewell of that beloved object, yet the impression of the man that hath been dear unto us, living an after-life in our memory, there putteth us in mind of further obsequies due unto the deceased. And namely of the performance of whatsoever we may judge shall make to his living credit, and to the affecting of his determination prevented by the stroke of death.
> By these meditations (as by an intellectual will) I suppose myself executor to the unhappily deceased author of this Poem, upon whom knowing that in his lifetime you bestowed many kind favours, entertaining the parts of reckoning and worth which you found in him, with good countenance and liberal affection. . . . I present the same to your most favourable allowance, offering my utmost self, now and ever to be ready, at your Worship's disposing:
>
> Edward Blount.

Edward Blount, then (in 1598, at least), accepted the story of Marlowe's death. Blount was to publish in 1609 the Quarto of *Pericles,* the title page of which affirmed that the drama was written by: William Shakespeare.

Pericles, expatiated upon earlier in this book, although not included in the First Folio of 1623, has gradually earned acceptance into the canonical dramas by virtue of an inimitable literary style recognized in it by scholars. Blount also, as Sir Sidney Lee concluded, played a chief part in the production of the First Folio [i.e., in publishing it in 1623] [and] unlike his companions [i.e., his partners in the Folio enterprise] had a true taste in literature. He had been a friend and admirer of Marlowe . . . and upon Blount probably fell the chief labor of seeing the First Folio through the press.

Now, did George Chapman finish *Hero and Leander?* Did he complete Marlowe's poem?

There are conservative scholars who do not think so. The eminent Edmund Malone, assessing the style of both finished and unfinished versions of the poem, declares that

a hundred lines of authentic Marlowe lie imbedded in George Chapman's continuation of "Hero and Leander."

Another reputable scholar—one of Marlowe's biographers —Francis Cunningham, states:

In the episode of Teras and other portions of the fifth Sestiad, the higher hand of Marlowe seems to me easily discernable. . . . The last Sestiad [also] of "Hero and Leander" was written by the author of "Dr. Faustus."

At this point it is imperative to remember, as previously noted, that the 1600 edition of *Hero and Leander* did not credit George Chapman with any part of the poem, giving it entirely to Christopher Marlowe.

In passing, it is worth observing what other students have to say about the two love-poems—Shakespeare's *Venus and Adonis* and Marlowe's *Hero and Leander*—aside from the deadly parallelisms between the two works quoted earlier:

H. C. Bartlett: " 'Venus and Adonis' has a close resemblance in style to Marlowe's 'Hero and Leander.' "

Oliver Elton (in a lecture before the British Academy): " 'Venus and Adonis' and 'The Rape of Lucrece' are . . . in the Ovidian, Italianate decorative manner which Christopher Marlowe had practiced . . . [in *Hero and Leander*]

In Chapman's alleged continuation of *Hero and Leander,* which begins with the third Sestiad, there are sixteen lines (183-198) which defy explanation. They are as obscure as the bulk of the *Sonnets* of Shakespeare. Obscure, that is, unless regarded in terms of the imposture.

For sheer vagueness of meaning they are unmatched in literature. They are, too, like the lines quoted from *As You Like It,* irrelevant to the continuity of the story, and were written into the body of the work with premeditation:

> Then thou most strangely-intellectual fire,
> That proper to my soul hast power to inspire
> Her burning faculties, and with the wings
> Of thy unsphered flame visiteth the springs
> Of spirits immortal; Now (as swift as time
> Doth follow motion) find the eternal clime
> Of his free soul, whose living subject stood
> Up to the chin in the Pyerean flood,
> And drunk to me half this Musean story,
> Inscribing it to deathless memory:
> Confer with it, and make my pledge as deep,
> That neithers' draught be consecrate to sleep.
> Tell it how much his late desires I tender,
> If yet it know not, and to light surrender
> My soul's dark offspring, willing it should die
> To loves, to passions, and society.

The lines do not apply to Hero or Leander. Guesses have been hazarded, and the most popular one is that Chapman is revealing how Marlowe urged him to finish the poem—on the premise that Marlowe, being aware of his impending murder, hurriedly charged Chapman with the task. No one, we can agree, with the vision of an assassination staring him in the face would worry about having another writer complete a poem he had begun; not even Marlowe.

I cannot explain the lines: they are beautiful, and their interpretation is open to everyone. Herewith mine:

O most strange and sacred Muse of creation, that hast inspired my highest faculties with the reaching flames of my winged powers, vouchsafe to visit the haunts of souls immortal. O now—now—as swift as time or motion, lead me to the lost bliss of my former state, when, on the topmost hill of creative joy, I swelled, as a flood, with still unfinished work, of which this Musean poem, but partly completed at the time of my "murder," was but one example.

Unfinished, I dedicated it at the time to deathless memory, knowing not when I would resume it. Now that I have resolved upon its completion, woo me, O Muse, and make me vow an eternal pledge to neither sleep nor rest till I have finished what I was fated to do in my yesteryear of bliss.

Woo it, I pray, and whisper to the glorious figures in my poem my vow to dedicate myself to its completion. Finally, when concluded, I will surrender the poem—my soul's dark offspring—as dark and secret as my life up to this time—to the world of love, passion, and society.

Unless divined in the light of historic deception, the lines are hopelessly, instead of partly, incomprehensible. One thing is certain—they have nothing to do with the passions of Hero and Leander. As for the author's purpose in writing them, I have made it as clear as I can: but I must admit, along with all other students of the lines, that I do not entirely comprehend them.

But all this leads to the climax of another event which may affirm that Christopher Marlowe did complete the poem as well as certify that he was very much alive after 1593.

The second 1598 edition of *Hero and Leander,* which the title page states was "Begun by Christopher Marlowe; and finished by George Chapman," contained, you will remember, an additional four parts—a total of six Sestiads, of which Marlowe's share was two.

We have previously remarked that Marlowe's name in the title page was printed in larger and bolder type than Chapman's, despite the fact that Marlowe's was the smaller share of the poem. Marlowe's portion of the poem, as we have seen, was prefaced with a dedication to his patron by Edward Blount, which I have already given.

As a foreword to the section where Chapman's writing commences, there is printed a Dedication addressed to Lady Walsingham—Sir Thomas's wife—written by George Chapman. The Dedication is astonishing enough to be reproduced here in full:

TO MY BEST ESTEEMED
and worthily honoured
LADY, THE LADY WALSINGHAM
one of the Ladies of her Majesties
    Bed-chamber.

I present your Ladyship with the last affections of the first two Lovers that ever Muse shrined in the Temple of Memory; being drawn by strange instigation to employ some of my serious time in so trifling a subject which yet made the first author, divine Musaeus, eternal. And were it not that we must subject our accounts of these commonly received conceits to servile custom, it goes much against my hand to sign that for a trifling subject, on which more worthiness of soul hath been showed, and weight of divine wit, than can vouchsafe residence in the leaden gravity of any Money-Monger, in whose profession all serious subjects are concluded. But he that shuns trifles, must shun the world, out of whose reverend heaps of substance and austerity, I can, and will, ere long, single, or tumble out as brainless and passionate fooleries as ever panted in the bosom of the most ridiculous Lover.

Accept it therefore good Madam, though as a trifle, yet as a serious argument of my affections; for to be thought thankful for all free and honourable favours, is a great sum of riches my whole thrift intendeth.

Such uncourtly and silly dispositions as mine, whose contentment hath other objects than profit or glory, are as glad, simply for the naked merit of virtue, to honour such as advance her, as others that are hired to commend with deepest politic bounty.

It hath, therefore, adjoined much contentment to my desire of your true honour to hear men of desert in Court add to mine own knowledge of your noble disposition; how gladly you do your best to prefer their desires, and have an absolute respect to their mere good parts, as if they came perfumed and charmed with golden incitements.

And this most sweet inclination, that flows from the truth and eternity of Nobles, assure your Ladyship doth more suit your other Ornaments, and makes more to the advancement of your name, and happiness of your proceedings, than if, like others, you displayed your ensigns of state and sourness in your forehead, made smooth with nothing but sensuality and presents.

This poor Dedication, in figure of the other unity betwixt Sir Thomas and yourself, hath rejoined you with him, my honoured best friend, whose continuance of ancient kindness to my still-obscured estate, though it cannot increase my love to him, which hath ever been entirely circular, yet shall it encourage my deserts to their utmost requital, and make my hearty gratitude speak; to which the unhappiness of my life hath hitherto been uncomfortable and painful dumbness.

By your Ladyship's vowed in
most wished service:
George Chapman.

Let us examine the portions of this astounding dedication cognate to our purpose:

In the first place, had George Chapman truly written the entire Dedication quoted above, then he must be pronounced an ingrate and a rascal, since he fails to credit or mention in any instance, by reference or directly, the poet Christopher Marlowe, who was not only solely responsible for the conception of *Hero and Leander,* but who actually wrote a sizable portion of the very poem that Chapman ostensibly finished.

If Marlowe requested Chapman to finish the poem before his foreknown murder (as scholars insist), would it not be reasonable to suppose that Chapman would refer in some way to Marlowe, especially since by the time of Chapman's Dedication, Marlowe was already dead, and certainly when the dedicatee was the wife of Marlowe's best friend and stanchest patron—Sir Thomas Walsingham.

Strangely enough, the one person whom Chapman should, as it were, have invoked from the "grave"—the one single person responsible for Chapman's having spent "more worthiness of soul" and "weight of divine wit" on the poem—is not anywhere, or at any time, by him mentioned.

Why would Chapman have been "drawn by strange instigation" to the task of continuing what Marlowe had begun? What was the compulsion? Why couldn't Chapman have hinted in the Dedication to Lady Walsingham that Marlowe —her husband's protégé—had asked him to complete the poem?

What was this powerful "instigation"?

There was none—for Chapman. There was one—a strong one—for Marlowe, if the argument of this book is applied to this Dedication of Chapman's.

The writer speaks of the first author, the "divine Musaeus," who first wrote of the Hero and Leander myth. Would it not have been incumbent upon Chapman to mention Marlowe, too?

The author of the Dedication sees fit to divulge to Lady Walsingham his hopes:

> I can, and will ere long . . . tumble out as brainless and passionate fooleries as ever panted in the bosom of the most ridiculous Lover.

In the light of the above quotation, it is necessary to point out that soon after the publication date of *Hero and Leander* (1598) Shakespeare began to tumble out comedies that were built on the "fooleries . . . of the most ridiculous Lover(s)."

Sir Sidney Lee, in his *A Life of William Shakespeare,* observed:

> In 1599 [i.e., one year after the Dedication had been written] Shakespeare . . . addressed himself to the composition of his

three most perfect essays in comedy—"Much Ado About Nothing," "As You Like It," and "Twelfth Night."

Chapman then makes the following comment:

... but he that shuns trifles, must shun the world; ... to be ... thankful for ... favours is ... a sum ... my whole thrift [i.e., effort] ... intendeth.

Hamlet in a somber mood comments on the state of the world:

Ay, sir; to be honest, as this world goes, is to be one man picked out of ten thousand.

Not a devastating parallelism; but a parallel utterance, certainly.

The last paragraph of the Dedication is the most astonishing one:

This poor Dedication, in figure of [i.e., in the image of] the other unity betwixt Sir Thomas and yourself.

He then describes Walsingham as

... my honoured best friend, whose continuance of ancient kindness to my still-obscured estate, though it cannot increase my love to him ... yet shall ... make my hearty gratitude speak; to which the unhappiness of my life hath hitherto been uncomfortable and painful dumbness.

Surely, this is Marlowe's agonizing voice, as he comments on Walsingham whose "continuance of ancient kindness to my still-obscured estate, though it cannot increase my love to him ... yet shall ... make my hearty ... gratitude speak."

Surely this is Marlowe's voice, crying out against his unhappy, painful dumbness:

... to which the unhappiness of my life hath hitherto been uncomfortable and painful dumbness.

The world saw George Chapman's signature. But it is Christopher Marlowe's voice that cries out, half hidden, from the protection of the Dedication.

I must ask, in all candor, whether George Chapman would have permitted his name to be inscribed as auxiliary author to *Hero and Leander,* and to the Dedication, had he never written what was assigned to him. Would he have permitted such fraudulent use of his name?

Replying with equal candor, remember that William Shakespeare permitted his name or initials to be inscribed in the title pages of eight Quarto dramas, all printed and published at the height of the author's powers—and seven of which have been rejected by Shakespearean authorities as fraudulent.

Did William Shakespeare take steps to prevent publication, or deny reponsibility for the fraudulent plays after they were printed?

He did not.

Neither did Chapman.

I believe the sole reason for inscribing George Chapman's name to *Hero and Leander* was the incriminatory Dedication Marlowe had penned, and which, in the nature of things as they existed, could never be attributed to our allegedly dead poet.

Scholars, as I have noted, have committed themselves to the belief that Marlowe did indeed write a good part of Chapman's continuation of *Hero and Leander.* Marlowe must, of necessity, have written the Dedication, since Chapman's ascription in the Dedication is based on the premise that Chapman had completed *Hero and Leander.* Bear in mind also that the 1600 edition of *Hero and Leander,* which, though it contained both unfinished and finished versions of the poem, did not ascribe a single word to George Chapman, but gave the entire credit to Christopher Marlowe. Was this a premeditated "error"?

Many of the parallelisms at the back of this book have been extracted from the poems of Shakespeare and from Marlowe's portion of *Hero and Leander*. Here are some specific samples:

Shakespeare's *Venus and Adonis:*
  Died to kiss his shadow in the brook.

Marlowe's *Hero and Leander:*
  . . . leaped into the water for a kiss
  Of his own shadow.

———————

Shakespeare's *Rape of Lucrece:*
  Her breasts, like ivory globes circled with blue,
  A pair of maiden worlds unconquered.

Marlowe's *Hero and Leander:*
  For though the rising ivory mount he scaled
  Which is with azure circling lines empaled,
  Much like a globe . . . may I term this.

*   *   *

  Wherein Leander on her quivering breast . . .

Many more parallelisms between the poems have been quoted and many more exist. But it is striking that an infinitely greater number have been found between George Chapman's alleged continuation of the poem and the Works of William Shakespeare, of which the following two partially illustrate the point:

Chapman's version of Marlowe's *Hero and Leander:*
  Come, come, dear night! Love's mart of kisses,
  Sweet close of his ambitious line,
  The fruitful summer of his blisses!
  Love's glory doth in darkness shine.
  O come, soft rest of cares,
  Come, night! Come, naked virtue's only tire,
  The reaped harvest of the light,
  Bound up in sheaves of sacred fire.
  Come, night, and lay thy velvet hand
  On glorious days outfacing face,
  And all thy crowned flames command,
  For torches to our nuptial night.

167

Shakespeare's *Romeo and Juliet* (to her lover on their nuptial
   night):
   Spread thy close curtain, love-performing night!

     *   *   *

   Leap into these arms, untalked and unseen.
   Lovers can see to do their amorous rites,
   . . . or if love be blind,
   It best agrees with night. Come, civil night,

     *   *   *

   And learn me how to lose a winning match,
   Played for with a pair of stainless maidenheads.

     *   *   *

   Come, night; come, Romeo—come thou day in night;

     *   *   *

   Come, gentle night—come, loving black-browed night,
   Give me my Romeo.

———————

Chapman's version of Marlowe's *Hero and Leander:*
   On glorious days outfacing face.

Shakespeare's *Love's Labour's Lost:*
   We have given thee faces, but you have outfaced them all.

It is more than likely that Christopher Marlowe wrote
both the finished version of *Hero and Leander* and the Dedicatory Epistle to Lady Walsingham. This, then, would be the
only single prose specimen that reveals the soul of the author
of the First Folio dramas and poems—a valuable contribution to the understanding of a great genius.

20

IN THE year 1600—seven years after Marlowe's alleged assassination—Lucan's *First Book,* translated line for line by Christopher Marlowe, was published in London by Thomas Thorpe. It was registered with the Stationers Company, September 28, 1593—the same day that *Hero and Leander* was registered. This is the same Thomas Thorpe who published Shakespeare's *Sonnets* in 1609; who condemned a baffled world to ignorance by failing to identify the mysterious Mr. W. H.'s identity.

We have seen how Walsingham qualifies as Thorpe's mystery dedicatee.

Just as enigmatic as was Thorpe's dedication of the *Sonnets* is his dedication of Marlowe's translation of Lucan; unless, again, interpreted in the light of the imposture. Having published Marlowe's translation of Lucan, Thorpe prefixed it with an Epistle Dedicatory. He addressed his dedication to Edward Blount, publisher of Marlowe's *Hero and Leander,* who in turn dedicated that poem to Marlowe's patron, Thomas Walsingham.

Sir Sidney Lee observed in his *Life of Shakespeare* that the *Sonnets* were "surreptitiously sent to the press" (by Thomas Thorpe) and, further, that "Thomas Thorpe made in 1600 his earliest hit by bringing to light Marlowe's translation of the 'First Book of Lucan'—just as, nine years later (1609), he similarly brought to light the 154 Sonnets of Shakespeare.

Where did Thorpe obtain the manuscript of Marlowe's translation? Where did he procure the manuscript of Shakespeare's *Sonnets*? Is it not possible that the same person supplied him with both manuscripts? And who might that person be?

Edward Blount, perhaps, well-known publisher—and friend of Marlowe's—or Sir Thomas Walsingham, who preserved each "trifle" of Marlowe's when that poet fled England in haste and "swift extremity"; an allusion made later by the author of Sonnet 48:

How careful was I when I took my way,
Each trifle [i.e., play or poem] under truest bars to thrust,
That, to my use, it might unused stay,
From hands of falsehood, in sure wards of trust.

These trifles—did Walsingham hold on to them and then dispose of them at the right time to publishers like Blount and Thorpe, whom he might trust?

There is evidence that Walsingham mingled with the stationers and publishers who either congregated or maintained their establishments in and around St. Paul's Churchyard. Documentary evidence, in fact. A record—a deposition sworn to by one William Smith, dated November 12, 1582—states that Smith, a publisher, lived for years in the Churchyard and that he was well known to Thomas Walsingham.

Walsingham, in point of fact, was friendly with several publishers, and must have been an impressive figure in London literary circles where he might conceivably have first met Marlowe, and where he undoubtedly associated with Blount and Thorpe.

And now Thorpe's dedication:

TO HIS KIND, AND TRUE FRIEND:
EDWARD BLOUNT

BLOUNT:
I purpose to be blunt with you, and out of my dullness to encounter you with a Dedication in the memory of that pure elemental Wit, Christopher Marlowe, whose Ghost or Genius is

to be seen walk the Churchyard in, at the least, three or four sheets. Methinks you should presently look wild now, and grow humourously frantic upon the test of it.

Well, least you should, let me tell you.

This Spirit was sometimes a familiar of your own, Lucans first book translated; which, in regard to your old right in it, I have raised in the circle of your patronage. But stay now, Edward, if I mistake not, you are to accommodate yourself with some few instructions, touching the property of a patron, that you are not yet possessed of; and to study them for your better grace as our gallants do fashions.

First, you must be proud and think you have merit enough in you, though you were ne'er so empty; then when I bring you the book, take physic, and keep state, assign me a time by your man to come again, and afore the day, be sure you have changed your lodging; in the meantime, sleep little, and sweat with the invention of some pitiful dry jest or two, which you may happen to utter, with some little, or not at all, marking of your friends, when you have found a place for them to come in at; or if by chance something from you has dropped worth the taking up, weary all that come to you with the repetition of it.

Censure scornfully enough, and somewhat like a travailer; commend nothing least you discredit your judgment.

These things, if you can, mould yourself to them Ned. I make no question but they will not become you. One special virtue in our Patrons of these days I have promised myself you shall fit excellently, which is to give nothing.

Yes, thy love I will challenge as my peculiar object both in this, and, I hope, in many more succeeding offices.

Farewell. I affect not the world should measure my thoughts to thee by a scale of this nature: Leave to think good of me when I fall from thee.

Thine in all rites of perfect friendship,

Thom. Thorpe.

What in heaven's name did Thorpe mean when he addressed Marlowe's friend, Edward Blount,

with a Dedication in the memory of that pure elemental Wit, Christopher Marlowe, whose Ghost or Genius is to be seen walk the Churchyard in, at the least, three or four sheets?

In context, is Thorpe referring to Marlowe's ghost? Or to Marlowe himself, Marlowe in the flesh, who can be seen walking the Churchyard in "three or four sheets" much like a Ghost indeed?

Could Marlowe have returned to London by 1600, in disguise, and, in disguise, walked his former paths as in bygone days? Thorpe would certainly not reveal the deception in dangerous print. The Dedication, therefore, is a delightful metaphor—a pun, if you will. It can be interpreted as saying that Marlowe's genius could be seen in "three or four sheets," that is, printer's broadsheets, hovering amidst the stalls of the Churchyard.

This was obviously what the general reader would see in the Dedication.

But for him who has eyes to see, and ears to hear, the Dedication has different connotations.

Why did Thorpe speak as he did? I believe he was tweaking Blount, because Blount, having become privy to the imposture (perhaps through Walsingham), withheld the exciting intelligence from his publisher friend, Thorpe.

And when Thorpe discovered the truth, he might well have parodied the imposture in planned metaphor.

Now, what did Thorpe mean by cautioning Blount thus:

> Methinks you should presently look wild now, and grow . . . frantic upon the test of it?

"Look wild" and "grow frantic"—"upon the test of" what? Why "wild"? Why "frantic"? Why "test"? Because, readers, if Blount knew what Thorpe already knew—after testing the truth that Marlowe's ghost, or Marlowe himself, had been seen walking the Churchyard, Blount indeed would quickly "grow frantic" at the knowledge Thorpe possessed. Indeed, he would be nothing less than wild and frantic! The secret was not only Walsingham's or Blount's now, but Thomas Thorpe's also.

Though the Dedication was abstruse enough to justify Thorpe's last paragraph—"Farewell. I affect not the world should measure my thoughts to thee by a scale of this nature"—it had one virtue: it served to prepare the world for another cryptic performance by the whimsical publisher.

21

WE NOW approach the last rampart of belief, to which all defenders of Shakespeare's authorship eventually retreat: the First Folio of 1623. Before 1623 doubts may have arisen, and facts may have shattered some of the cherished conceptions of the life and work of William Shakespeare; the First Folio stands inviolate, banishing all doubts as to the reality of William Shakespeare.

Or does it?

When the First Folio was published, most of the thirty-six plays it contained had never been produced in the London theaters. Someone, therefore, must have gathered together these plays, published and unpublished.

The record reveals that five men formed a partnership, for the purpose of printing and publishing the thirty-six plays. It was a major financial undertaking for the times. The volume was unusually large by early-seventeenth century standards. The tallest extant copy measures 13⅜ x 8½ inches and contains 908 pages. The text is printed in two columns with 66 lines to the column. The estimate of printing runs close to 500 copies, of which approximately 185 survive. Running counter to prevailing custom, sixteen of the twenty unpublished plays were registered with the Stationers Company almost as soon as the printing of the Folio had been completed. The date was November 8, 1623. On that day Edward Blount and Isaac Jaggard registered the dramas in their names, and shortly afterwards they received license to publish the volume. The practice of the day was to first register a work and then, eventually, to bring out the book. The procedure in this case was strangely reversed.

The five men that formed the publishing syndicate were William Jaggard; Isaac Jaggard, his son; William Aspley; John Smethwick; and Edward Blount, Christopher Marlowe's friend and admirer. The Jaggards were professional printers, the only ones of the quintet. Aspley and Smethwick were publishers and booksellers only, of no great reputation in their field but already known as speculators in a few Shakespearean plays.

Of Edward Blount, the noted biographer Sir Sidney Lee had this to say:

> The publisher Edward Blount . . . played a chief part in the production of the First Folio. . . . unlike his companions [he] had a true taste in literature. He had been a friend and admirer of Christopher Marlowe and had actively engaged in the posthumous publication of two of Marlowe's poems. . . . Upon Blount fell the chief labor of seeing the work [i.e., the First Folio] through the press.

Behind these five men (Blount was the midwife to the volume) there was a guiding hand: a hand that had supplied the plays to the publishers. In the light of what my argument has revealed—this guiding hand could have been no other than that of Sir Thomas Walsingham; who not only gave the plays to the syndicate, but must have preserved them as Marlowe wrote them, from wherever the poet might be.

We have seen how there is documentary evidence attesting to Walsingham's familiarity with the publishers of St. Paul's Churchyard. We have recorded his intimacy with Edward Blount. Where and when Marlowe eventually died, there is no way of knowing; his second death would have been kept as much a secret as his first escape; but certainly Walsingham and Blount would have been more than eager to keep their friend's memory alive. What better way than to immortalize his "trifles" with a monumental publication, a Folio edition of his works?

The First Folio was printed during the year 1623 at the press in the Barbican, which the Jaggards owned. The title page reads as follows:

Mr. William
SHAKESPEARES's
Comedies,
Histories, &
Tragedies
Published according to the True Original Copies.

The page also includes a large engraving of Shakespeare, executed by Martin Droeshout, of London.

The Epistle Dedicatory addressed to the Earls of Pembroke and Montgomery is signed by John Heming and Henry Condell, two men known as performers in William Shakespeare's acting company. This is followed by another address, "To the great Variety of Readers," again signed by John Heming and Henry Condell.

Commendatory verses are supplied by Ben Jonson, Hugh Holland, Leonard Digges, and someone who signs himself "J. M." and whose identity has been the subject of much conjecture. Likely all were poets—Jonson certainly—since the verses are for the most part competent.

Following this comes "The Names of the Principal Actors in all these Plays"—twenty-six in all—headed by William Shakespeare. A "Catalogue" follows, of all the plays contained in the volume, with one exception—*Troilus and Cressida*—which, although it is not catalogued, is nevertheless printed in the book.

Herewith the prefatory matter, with commentary:

and

WILLIAM

Earl of Pembroke, &c. Lord Chamberlain to the
King's Most Excellent Majesty

and

PHILIP

Earl of Montgomery, &c. Gentleman of his Majesties
Bed-Chamber.

Both Knights of the most Noble Order of the Garter,
and our singular good Lords.

Right Honourable,

Whilst we study to be thankful in our particular for the
many favours we have received from your L. L. we are fallen
upon the ill fortune, to mingle two the most diverse things
that can be, fear, and rashness: rashness in the enterprize, and
fear of the success. For, when we value the places your H.H.
sustain, we cannot but know their dignity greater, then to
descend to the reading of these trifles: and, while we name
them trifles, we have deprived ourselves of the Defence of our
Dedication. But since your L. L. have been pleased to think
these trifles something, heretofore; and have prosecuted both
them, and their Author living, with so much favour: we hope,
that (they out-living him, and he not having the fate, common
with some, to be executor of his own writings) you will use the
like indulgence toward them you have done unto their parent.

There is a great difference, whether any Book choose his
Patrons, or find them: This hath done both. For, so much were
your L. L. likings of the several parts, when they were acted
as before they were published, the Volume asked to be yours.

We have but collected them, and done an office to the dead
to procure his Orphans, Guardians: without ambition either of
self-profit, or fame: only to keep the memory of so worthy a
Friend, & Fellow alive, as was our Shakespeare, by humble offer
of his Plays, to your most noble patronage. Wherein, as we
have justly observed, no man to come near your L. L. but with
a kind of religious address: it hath been the height of our care,
who are the Presenters, to make the present worthy of your
H. H. by the perfection.

177

But, there we must also crave our abilities to be considered, my Lords. We cannot go beyond our own powers. Country hands reach forth milk, cream, fruits, or what they have: and many Nations (we have heard) that had not gums & incense obtained their requests with a leavened Cake. It was no fault to approach their Gods by what means they could: And the most, though meanest, of things are made more precious, when they are dedicated to Temples.

In that name therefore, we most humbly consecrate to your H. H. these remains of your servant Shakespeare; that what delight is in them, may be ever your L. L. the reputation his, & the faults ours, if any be committed, by a pair so careful to show their gratitude both to the living, and the dead, as is

Yours Lordships most bounden,

John Heming
Henry Condell

Heming and Condell revealed in this dedication their friendship with their fellow actor. They themselves stated in the Dedication that their only contribution to the Folio consisted in "collecting" the plays as a duty to the dead author and to procure for these plays Guardians, or publishers.

That is all that these two actors ever had to do with the volume.

However, more than one-third of the dramas printed had been neither published, nor produced in London theaters. How did Heming and Condell, then, collect the unpublished plays? And from whom?

The actors in question did not receive these unpublished and unproduced plays from Shakespeare; had they, there would have been no need to collect them at all. And they would undoubtedly have mentioned the fact that Shakespeare had handed them the dramas.

Further, their statement that they had "collected" them certainly implies that they had collected them all. This is patently untrue, since no less than twenty of the plays—

sixteen authentic plays and four source plays—had been previously published in Quarto and were accessible to anyone who wished to buy them; they were available to publishers like Blount, the Jaggards, Smethwick, and Aspley—who, with their stature, did not need to rely upon two actors to collect for their undertaking books already printed and long in circulation.

Why, then, were Heming and Condell so careful to state in their dedication that they had "collected them"—collected all of the thirty-six dramas—when they had done no such thing?

As Sir Sidney Lee concluded, in his *Life of William Shakespeare,*:

> The two actors made pretension to a larger responsibility for the enterprise than they really had incurred.

It is important to remember that both Heming and Condell were actors; and that nothing much else is known of them. Heming ended his days as a grocer, while Condell, in the last period of his life, became a publican. Condell died in 1623, probably before it was possible for him to see the Folio Edition come off the press. His colleague lived seven years longer—until 1630. Both men were in their sixties when they died.

There is nothing wrong with being a pub owner or a grocer. But, granted the educational limitations of the Elizabethan period, is it possible for two such tradesmen to have penned the highly learned Dedication to Peers of the Realm —especially when these actors were at the time behind counters?

And why do I say, a "learned dedication"? Because the bulk of their address to the Noblemen is a most ingenious paraphrase of Pliny's Latin classic, *Natural History,* as the following parallelization reveals:

For, when we value the places your H.H. sustain, we cannot but know their dignity greater, then to descend to the reading of these trifles.

Wherein, as we have justly observed, no man to come near your L. L. but with a kind of religious address; it hath been the height of our care, who are the Presenters, to make the present worthy of your H.H. by the perfection.

Country hands reach forth milk, cream, fruits, or what they have: and many Nations (we have heard) that had not gums & incense obtained their requests with a leavened cake. It was no fault to approach their Gods by what means they could.

And the most, though meanest, of things are made more precious when they are dedicated to Temples.

And, while we name them trifles, we have deprived ourselves of the Defence of our Dedication.

But since your L. L. have been pleased to think these trifles something, heretofore; and have prosecuted both them, and their author living,

I considered your situation much too elevated for you to descend to such an office.

. . . even those who come to pay their respects to you do so with a kind of veneration: on this account I ought to be careful that what is dedicated to you should be worthy of you.

But the country people, and indeed, some whole nations offer milk to the Gods, and those who cannot procure frankincense substitute in its place salted cakes, for the Gods are satisfied when they are worshipped by everyone to the best of his ability.

. . . for things are often conceived to be of great value, solely because they are consecrated in temples.

And by this dedication I have deprived myself of the benefit of challenge. For still thou ne'er wouldst quite despise the trifles that I write.

For it is a very different thing whether a person has a judge given him by lot, or whether he voluntarily selects one.

with so much favour. . . .
There is a great difference,
whether any Book choose his
Patrons, or find them: This
hath done both.

Would such men as Condell and Heming have saturated
themselves with the writings of a famous Latin classicist to
the extent of being able adroitly to reproduce whole passages
from his work in a dedication to a book of plays?

Appleton Morgan, editor of the *Bankside Shakespeare,* puts
it aptly indeed:

Such a deadly parallel column . . . sufficiently indicates that
"Heming and Condell" is a pseudonym for someone who was
very much another sort of person from the two actors who
ended their days as a grocer and a publican.

Again, the fact that the two actors names are signed to the
Dedication is no guarantee that they composed it. We have
amply demonstrated that literary ethics in Elizabethan times
were not of the highest; and if William Shakespeare could
sign his name to plays that were not his, certainly two actors
could lend their names to a dedication.

Who, then, is the real author of the Dedication? We do not
know. It might have been one of the publishers involved in
the Folio enterprise—Edward Blount, who, as Sir Sidney
Lee conceded, "had a true taste in literature," is a strong
possibility.

As to the reason why John Heming and Henry Condell
were used, it was to reinforce the masquerade: the tale of
Shakespeare's authorship of Christopher Marlowe's works;
a tale which an Address, signed by two of Shakespeare's
known friends and fellow actors, would vigorously substantiate and fortify.

Hard upon the Pembroke-Montgomery Dedication, another inscription by Heming and Condell appears in the Folio, which it would be well to quote in full:

To the Great Variety of Readers.—From the most able to him that can but spell; . . . there you are numbered. We had rather you were weighed, especially when the fate of all books depends upon your capacities, and not your heads alone, but of your purses. Well! It is now public, and you will stand for your priviliges we know; to read and censure. Do so, but buy it first. That doth best commend a book, the stationer says.

Then, how odd soever your brains be, or your wisdoms, make your license the same and spare not. Judge your sixpence worth, your shillings worth, your five shillings worth at a time, or higher, so you rise to the just rates, and welcome.

But, whatever you do, buy. Censure will not drive a trade or make the jack go. And though you be a magistrate of wit, and sit on the stage at Black-Friars or the Cock-pit to arraign plays daily, know, these plays have had their trial already, and stood out all appeals, and do now come forth quitted rather by a Decree of Court than any purchased letters of commendation.

It had been a thing, we confess, worthy to have been wished, that the author himself had lived to have set forth and overseen his own writings; but since it hath been ordained otherwise, and he by death departed from that right, we pray you do not envy his friends the office of their care and pain to have collected and published them; and so to have published them, as where, before, you were abused with diverse stolen and surreptitious copies, maimed and deformed by the frauds and stealths of injurious imposters that exposed them; even those are now offered to your view cured and perfect of their limbs, and all the rest absolute in their numbers as he conceived them; who, as he was a happy imitator of Nature, was a most gentle expresser of it.

His mind and hand went together; and what he thought, he uttered with that easiness that we have scarce received from him a blot in his papers.

But it is not our province, who only gather his works and give them you, to praise him. It is yours that read him. And there, we hope, to your divers capacities, you will find enough both to draw and hold you; for his wit can no more lie hid then it could be lost.

Read him, therefore; and again and again; and if then you do not like him, surely you are in some manifest danger not to understand him.

And so we leave you to other of his friends, whom, if you need, can be your guides. If you need them not, you can lead yourselves and others; and such readers we wish him—John Heming—Henry Condell.

This commercial appeal is the province of the publisher, as it has been for centuries, and still is today. Why should this syndicate of five men, each of whom was highly successful and knowledgeable in his field, find it necessary to call upon John Heming and Henry Condell—actor-tradesmen—to write the only advertisement in the enormously expensive and important First Folio?

What qualified this grocer and this publican for such a task?

Nothing.

Whoever it was who caused their names to be subscribed to the introductory matter was interested only in establishing a connection between the two actors and William Shakespeare; a further effort to make the imposture as lifelike, as airtight, as possible.

The device was successful enough to deceive scholars to this day; and learned Elizabethan experts are still eulogizing Heming and Condell as the "editors" of the Shakespeare Folio.

Which, of course, is what had been originally planned almost four hundred years ago.

There are, of course, some statements made in the Address to "Readers" which impute the honesty of these two former actors—assuming that they actually wrote the Address assigned them.

They proclaim:

. . . these plays have had their trial already, and stood out all appeals, and do now come forth quitted rather by a Decree of Court than any purchased letters of commendation.

How could Heming and Condell say that the plays had had their trial already, when nearly two-thirds of them were not published at all, and more than one-third of them never, to all intent and purpose, were produced and were not known even to have existed at the time, save perhaps for some few fortunate and knowledgeable mortals?

The statement must of necessity be a lie.

Heming and Condell assert in their second inscription that they exercised "care and pain to have collected and published them." Yet in the first inscription they state: "We have but collected them."

An inconsistency, to say the least.

And again:

After having asserted that they "collected and published them," a few sentences later they speak of themselves as those "who only gather his works."

And now the crowning misstatement of all:

> . . . where, before, you were abused with diverse stolen and surreptitious copies, maimed and deformed by the fraud and stealths of injurious imposters that exposed them; even those are now offered to your view cured and perfect of their limbs, and all the rest absolute in their numbers as he conceived them . . .

Not even the most conservative of Shakespearean scholars believes this particular declaration. Here is what a few of them have to say about this statement:

> Edmund Malone: ". . . instead of printing these plays from manuscripts, the editors, to save labor, or from some other motive, printed the greater part of them from the very quartos which Heming and Condell represented as 'maimed and imperfect.' "

> Charles F. Johnson: "Heming and Condell speak of the plays as 'stolen and surreptitious copies.' . . . Although they stigmatized all the quartos as 'stolen,' in many cases the quartos are fuller than the same plays in the Folio."

> Sir Sidney Lee: "The boastful advertisement of Heming and

Condell that they had access to Shakespeare's papers . . . admits of no literal interpretation."

W. A. Neilson and A. H. Thorndike: "It is well to be cautious in accepting at its face value the implication contained in their [i.e., Heming and Condell's] words."

The statement that the plays "are now offered to your view . . . absolute in their numbers as he conceived them" cannot be admitted as truth, even by the most conservative Shakespeareans. Sir Edmund K. Chambers sums up this sentiment:

> Internal evidence makes it necessary to accompany a general acceptance of the traditional Shakespeare Canon [i.e., chiefly on the basis of Heming and Condell's assertions] with certain qualifications.

This confession of fallibility of the sacrosanct First Folio is astonishing enough. But Sir Edmund (a most conservative and orthodox Shakespearean) does not rest there:

> Collaboration must be admitted in "Henry VIII" . . . in "The Taming of the Shrew," as well as in . . . "Pericles."

But Chambers is by no means the first Shakespearean scholar to doubt the authority of the First Folio. Alexander Pope, in 1725, admitted to doubts about *Comedy of Errors, Love's Labour's Lost,* and *The Winter's Tale.* In 1734, Lewis Theobald disavowed complete Shakespearean authorship of *Henry V;* Sir T. Hamner, in 1743, of *Two Gentlemen of Verona;* Samuel Johnson, in 1765, of *Richard II;* Dr. Richard Farmer, in 1767, of *The Taming of the Shrew.*

Men of the caliber of Edmund Malone, Samuel T. Coleridge, and J. O. Halliwell-Phillipps questioned the single authorship of the *Henry VI* trilogy and of *Titus Andronicus.* Coleridge was suspicious even of *Macbeth;* and F. G. Fleay and Dugdale Sykes questioned the authenticity of *Richard III.*

Of the moderns, C. F. Tucker Brooke and Thomas Marc

Parrott have wondered about the sole authorship of *Richard II* and *Henry VI*. William Wells and H. C. Oliphant have attacked the total ascription of *Julius Caesar*. Professor Dover Wilson, a citadel of orthodoxy, finds only four plays that he can, in all conscience, assign wholly to Shakespeare; while J. M. Robertson, as noted, doubts to greater or lesser degree the authorship of twenty of the Folio plays.

Georg Brandes, Danish literary critic, writes:

> The 1623 Folio . . . purports to be printed "according to the True Original Copies"; this assertion is demonstrably false in the numerous instances in which we can test it.

Dr. Brandes adds an afterthought that is singularly appropriate to the present theme:

> We do not know what made Shakespeare so careless of his fame as he seems to have been. We only know that he himself did not publish his dramatic works and that he does not even mention them in his will.

The other familiar boast made by Heming and Condell, that "we have scarce received from him [i.e., Shakespeare] a blot in his papers," is unworthy of extended commentary. First, they did not "receive" anything, but according to their own admission had only collected the works. Second, a goodly portion of sixteen Folio dramas were not printed from "his papers," that is, from the author's manuscripts—because the publishers reproduced their copy directly from the already extant Quartos.

It would be nothing less than a miracle if an author could present manuscripts to his publisher with "scarce" a blot or correction in them.

Even if my test is accepted, and a professional scrivener is admitted to have copied the texts of the plays, a hand as chaste as the one suggested by Messrs. Heming and Condell is still an impossibility—even for a professional calligrapher.

Sir Edmund Chambers summarizes Heming and Condell's ridiculous statement:

> We cannot . . . take quite literally the statement of Heming and Condell that they had scarce received a blot in Shakespeare's papers. It would be absurd to take it quite literally.

Since the statements of Heming and Condell are a tissue of lies, can it still be maintained that they were the authors of the Dedicatory Epistle and the Address "To the Great Variety of Readers"? Not with any confidence.

But, if not these two, who then? We have suggested, and the suggestion still stands, that Edward Blount, friend and admirer of Christopher Marlowe, a man with "a true taste in literature," could have been the author of both prefatory pieces. Granting this, he stands accused of all the animadversions cast upon Heming and Condell. In Blount's case, though, it is pardonable. He was, after all, a publisher. His aim was to stimulate the Folio's sales. And the misstatements and actual exaggerations would prove, if not forgivable, at least understandable.

No—there was certainly a plan afoot, when Shakespeare's fellow actors put their names to an Address which it is doubtful that they were even capable of writing.

22

WE return now to *Pericles*. Remember, Heming and Condell attested that the Folio incorporated all the plays "absolute in their numbers." And yet this First Folio, the bulwark of orthodox Shakespearean scholarship, did not contain the drama *Pericles*, which almost every editor and critic of the past two hundred fifty years (counter to the testimony of both Heming and Condell and of the First Folio itself) has accepted as a Shakespearean play.

If *Pericles* was written by the author of the First Folio, why, in that case, was it omitted from the Works? There is only one conclusion: *Pericles* was not written by the Folio author: but scholarship maintains that it was written by the author of the First Folio!

Again we meet the strange sophistry of the Shakespearean scholar.

Pericles is certainly the Achilles' heel of literary orthodoxy.

23

AND now we come to the famous Ben Jonson panegyric which immediately follows the Address "To the Great Variety of Readers." It is necessary here to set it down:

TO THE MEMORY OF MY BELOVED,
THE AUTHOR
Mr. William Shakespeare:
and
what he hath left us.

To draw no envy (Shakespeare) on thy name,
   Am I thus ample to thy Book, and Fame:
While I confess thy writings to be such,
   As neither Man, nor Muse, can praise too much,
'Tis true, and all men's suffrage. But these ways
   Were not the paths I meant unto thy praise:
For seeliest Ignorance on these may light,
   Which, when it sounds at best, but echo's right;
Or blind Affection, which doth ne're advance
   The truth, but gropes, and urgeth all by chance;
Or crafty malice, might pretend this praise,
   And think to ruin, where it seemed to raise.
These are, as some infamous bawd, or whore,
   Should praise a Matron. What could hurt her more?
But thou art proof against them, and indeed
   Above the ill fortune of them, or the need.
I, therefore, will begin. Soul of the Age!
   The applause! delight! the wonder of our Stage!
My Shakespeare, rise: I will not lodge thee by

Chaucer, or Spenser, or bid Beaumont lie
A little further, to make thee a room:
  Thou art a monument, without a tomb,
And art alive still, while thy Book doth live,
  And we have wits to read, and praise to give.
That I not mix thee so, my brain excuses
  I mean with great, but disproportioned Muses:
For, if I thought my judgment were of years,
  I should commit thee surely with thy peers,
And tell, how far thou didst our Lily out-shine,
  Or sporting Kyd, or Marlowe's mighty line.
And though thou hadst small Latin, and less Greek,
  From thence to honour thee, I would not seek
For names; but call forth thundering Aeschylus,
  Euripides, and Sophocles to us,
Paccuuius, Accius, him of Cordova dead,
  To life again, to hear thy Buskin tread,
And shake a stage: Or, when thy socks were on,
  Leave thee alone, for the comparison
Of all, that insolent Greece or haughty Rome
  Sent forth, or since did from their ashes come.
Triumph, my Britain, thou hast one to show,
  To whom all scenes of Europe homage owe.
He was not of an age, but for all time!
  And all the Muses still were in their prime.
When like Apollo he came forth to warm
  Our ears, or like a Mercury to charm!
Nature herself was proud of his designs,
  And joyed to wear the dressing of his lines!
Which were so richly spun, and woven so fit,
  As, since, she will vouchsafe no other Wit.
The merry Greek, tart Aristophanes,
  Neat Terrence, witty Plautus, now not please;
But antiquated, and deserted lie
  As they were not of Nature's family.
Yet must I not give Nature all: Thy art,
  My gentle Shakespeare, must enjoy a part.
For though the Poet's matter, Nature be,
  His art doth give the fashion. And that he,
Who casts to write a living line, must sweat,

(Such as thine are) and strike the second heat
Upon the Muses anvil: turn the same
    (And himself with it) that he thinks to frame;
Or for the laurel he may gain a scorn,
    For a good poet's made, as well as born.
And such wert thou. Look how the father's face
    Lives in his issue, even so, the race
Of Shakespeare's mind, and manners, brightly shines
    In his well turned, and true-filed lines;
In each of which, he seems to shake a lance,
    As brandished at the eyes of ignorance.
Sweet Swan of Avon! what a sight it were
    To see thee in our waters yet appear
And make those flights upon the banks of Thames,
    That so did take Eliza, and our James!
But stay, I see thee in the Hemisphere
    Advanced, and made a Constellation there!
Shine forth, thou Star of Poets, and with rage,
    Or influence, chide, or cheer the drooping stage;
Which, since thy flight from hence, hath mourned like night,
    And despairs day, but for thy Volumes light.

Ben: Jonson

A stately and beautiful compliment. But was Jonson sincere when he wrote of the First Folio author? It is my belief that he was not. His feelings were feigned, as I shall endeavor to prove.

Now, there is nothing in Ben Jonson's First Folio testimony of William Shakespeare that can substantiate Jonson's own knowledge of the London actor as a writer. Jonson's celebrated conversations with William Drummond of Hawthornden, on his visits to Scotland, were concerned only with the previously published plays and poems. While the talk of these two gentlemen drifted at times to criticism of Shakespeare's craftsmanship, it never centered around the author himself, and never stemmed from a personal knowledge of William Shakespeare as a writer.

Ben Jonson was, of course, ignorant of Marlowe's authorship and of the tremendous imposture that sustained such ignorance. Jonson believed, as all England believed, that Marlowe lay buried at Deptford.

The very fact that Ben Jonson was hired as chief elegist sealed Marlowe's fate in the world's eyes as compellingly as Heming and Condell's "Address" stamped Shakespeare's authorship of the Folio.

The hand that had planned the one planned the other. The tiny cracks in the structure of deceit were being calked, made as airtight as human ingenuity could make them.

It is a matter of record (to go into further detail) that Jonson for twenty years was regularly hired to write Dedications, Laudations, and Eulogies for books, pamphlets, individuals, and court matters. Jonson was the court poet of the reign of King James, the "glamor boy" of the early seventeenth century, lionized to an unusual degree. In fact, Jonson must have made a fair part of his very good living from the proceeds of his hired and complimentary pen.

It would be logical, then, for the publishers of the Folio to seek Jonson's services.

Publishers were no less sensitive to gain in Elizabethan times than they are today. We have concrete evidence of this —if evidence were needed: in the satire *Return from Parnassus,* Second Part, published about 1601, John Danter, an Elizabethan publisher of plays, is made to speak in this manner by its author:

> Danter: "I lost by your last book; and you know there is many a one that pays me largely for the printing of their inventions."

Jonson's elegy, then, was made to order—for money. There is nothing shameful in that. But Jonson's hypocrisy was truly odious. In 1630—just about seven years after his exquisite eulogy—Jonson wrote, in his *Timber, or Discoveries* (published posthumously in 1641), the following estimate of

William Shakespeare, whom he had so flattered less than a decade before:

> I remember the Players have often mentioned it as an honour to Shakespeare, that in his writing, whatsoever he penned, he never blotted out a line. [I.e., an obvious reference to the Heming and Condell statement that "we have scarce received from him a blot in his papers."]
>
> My answer hath been: would he had blotted a thousand. Which they thought a malevolent speech. I had not told posterity this, but for their ignorance, who chose that circumstance to commend their friend by [that] wherein he most faulted. ... He ... had ... expressions wherein he flowed with that facility that sometimes it was necessary he should be stopped.
>
> His wit was in his own power; would the rule of it had been so too. Many times he fell into those things [that] could not escape laughter, as, when he said, in the person of Caesar, one speaking to him: "Caesar, thou dost me wrong." He replied: "Caesar did never wrong but with just cause" and such like, which were ridiculous.

It is a matter of record that throughout Jonson's lifetime—he was Marlowe's junior by nine years—he jeered and damned all the plays he knew as Shakespeare's. He accused Shakespeare of being a scribbling barbarian, a violator of Aristotle's holy law of dramatic unities. Jonson, like the French dramatists, never ceased excoriating the Folio author for disregarding the trinity of action, time, and place.

Jonson, therefore, was a literary mercenary, hired to commend. For scholarship to turn to Ben Jonson's eulogy as "testimony" that the author of the Folio was William Shakespeare is ridiculous. Jonson would have written anything for money——

No wonder "George Chapman," who, as I have earlier submitted, might have been none other than Christopher Marlowe, in his Dedication to the wife of our poet's friend and patron, Sir Thomas Walsingham (which prefaced *Hero and Leander*), had this to say of the ilk and cast of venal Ben Jonson:

Such . . . dispositions as mine . . . are as glad, simply for the naked merit of virtue, to honour such as advance . . . her [i.e., virtue] as others that are hired to commend with deepliest politic [i.e., crafty] bounty.

Three other elegiacs prefaced the 1623 Folio. They were written by relatively obscure poets. There is no reason we know of why the publishers of the Folio chose these three men to preface the Folio, except that perhaps in this manner Shakespeare's authorship was made the more sound.

While we are concerned with but two of the three elegies, all follow below, for the sake of the record, in the order that they were published:

UPON THE LINES AND LIFE OF THE FAMOUS
SCENIC POET, MASTER WILLIAM SHAKESPEARE

Those hands, which you so clapped, go now, and wring
You Britains brave; for done are Shakespeare's days:
His days are done, that made the dainty Plays.
Which made the Globe of heaven and earth to ring.
Dried is that vein, dried is the Thespian Spring;
Turned all to tears, and Phoebus clouds his rays;
That corpse, that coffin now bestick those bayes,
Which crowned him Poet first, then Poet's King.
If Tragedies might any Prologue have,
All those he made, would scarce make one to this:
Where Fame, now that he gone is to the grave
(Deaths public tiring-house) the Nuncius is.
For though his line of life went soon about,
The life yet of his lines shall never out.

Hugh Holland

TO THE MEMORY
OF THE DECEASED AUTHOR MASTER
W. SHAKESPEARE

Shake-speare, at length thy pious fellows give
The world thy Works: thy Works, by which, out-live
Thy Tomb, thy name must: when that stone is rent,
And Time dissolves thy Stratford Monument,

Here we alive shall view thee still. This Book,
When Brass and Marble fade, shall make thee look
Fresh to all Ages: when Posterity
Shall loath what's new, think all is prodigy
That is not Shake-speares ev'ry line, each Verse
Here shall revive, redeem thee from thy Hearse.
Nor Fire, nor cankring Age, as Naso said,
Of his, thy wit-fraught Book shall once invade.
Nor shall I e're believe, or think thee dead
(Though mist) until our bankrupt Stage be sped
(Impossible) with some new strain t'out-do
Passions of Juliet, and her Romeo;
Or till I hear a Scene more nobly take,
Then when thy half-Sword parleying Romans spake.
Till these, till any of thy Volumes rest
Shall with more fire, more feeling be expressed,
Be sure, our Shake-speare, thou canst never die,
But crowned with Laurel, live eternally.

L. Digges

TO THE MEMORY OF M. W. SHAKE-SPEARE.

We wondered (Shake-speare) that thou went'st so soon
From the Worlds-Stage, to the Graves-Tiring-room.
We thought thee dead, but this thy printed worth,
Tells thy Spectators, that thou went'st but forth
To enter with applause. An Actors Art
Can die, and live, to act a second part.
That's but an Exit of mortality;
This, a Re-entrance to a Plaudity.

J. M.

Only two of these poems interest us here—Holland's and the one whose author signed himself J.M. Of Digges's lines, all that can be said is that the writer penned a sentimental appreciation to the writer of the Folio, whom he accepted as William Shakespeare.

It is an impersonal, though moving, expression; tantalizingly objective about the author of whom we want to know so much. It adds nothing to our information or knowledge of the author of the Canon. Thus, this elegy, like Jonson's, falls short of being "testimony" to Shakespeare's authorship of the Folio plays.

Now as to Hugh Holland. Consider these lines:

> For though his line of life went soon about
> The life yet of his lines shall never out.

Clearly this can only mean that the author's life ended early. Death, Holland tells us, came to the Folio author while he was still young. No other interpretation of the line is possible.

If we grant, for the moment, that Shakespeare did write the works ascribed to him, how can Holland write or infer that Shakespeare died young—or even relatively young?

Consider the documentary evidence. It attests to the fact that William Shakespeare died in his fifty-third year.

Could any Elizabethan be considered to have died young at the age of 52?

The life span of most Elizabethans, as we have seen in previous pages, fell far short of the half-century mark. Fifty-two, in Elizabethan times, was respectable, even unusual, old age. A man who died after his fiftieth year died a relatively old man.

Then, why did Holland speak of Shakespeare in this fashion when he knew that the author had died seven years earlier, in 1616, in the fullness of his time? The line takes on a strange aspect.

Holland was hired to write the elegy. Is it possible that he was instructed by Edward Blount, perhaps, to insert the line as a wry reflection on the true fate of Christopher Marlowe's "youngish" death?

24

LAST of all, we come to the lines of the writer who signed himself "J. M." It is conjectured that the initials were those of either James Mabbe, Jasper Maine, or some other unknown poet. The initials have never been identified.

Consider this:

> We wondered (Shake-speare) that thou went'st so soon
> From the Worlds-Stage, to the Graves-Tiring-room.
> We thought thee dead, but this thy printed worth,
> Tells thy spectators that thou went'st but forth
> To enter with applause. An Actors Art,
> Can die, and live, to act a second part.
> That's but an Exit of mortality;
> This, a Re-entrance to a Plaudity.

If these words are considered in the light of our thesis, they take on strange and fascinating significance!

> We wondered (Shake-speare) that thou went'st so soon.

The voice of Hugh Holland echoes in this line. J. M., strangely enough, also wondered why the Folio author "went so soon":

> From the Worlds-Stage, to the Graves-Tiring-room.

J. M. indeed wondered that the Author departed life's stage "so soon" for the "tiring-room" of death. Indeed, it was strange and pitiful that Marlowe (for J. M. is obviously referring to Marlowe, and not to William Shakespeare) died so early a death, in 1593.

And then:

> We thought thee dead . . .

Yes, J. M. thought Christopher Marlowe had died at Deptford.

> . . . but this thy printed worth,
> Tells thy Spectators, that thou went'st but forth
> To enter with applause.

I paraphrase: The world, Marlowe, having thought thee dead, this volume tells your public you departed life only to re-enter it with greater applause than was yours originally when you left life in 1593.

> . . . An Actors Art
> Can die, and live to act a second part.
> That's but an Exit of mortality . . .

Though a great actor dies, yet his art lives on, in the efforts of another actor, who plays again the play of his predecessor. Thus, "an Actors Art can die, and live, to act a second part."

But you, Marlowe, your exit from mortality is:

> . . . a Re-entrance to a Plaudity.

For your return to the world of the living was a rebirth— a re-entrance—to greater acclaim than you had ever known before.

The question will be asked, did Edward Blount or Marlowe's patron, Sir Thomas Walsingham, allow this revelation of their thirty-year-old secret to be printed, for all the world to read? The answer must be that, like all successful plotters, they were overconfident. Heming and Condell, Ben Jonson— the title page itself—and Leonard Digges, all these were seals which forever locked the story of the impostor from public knowledge. They permitted themselves, secure in their cleverness, an oblique avowal of Marlowe's authorship —one of the subtle puns the Elizabethans loved so; and the pun, the subtle thrust, was delivered by J. M., as he wrote his lines.

We are led to the conclusion, after all this, that the prefatory matter of the First Folio actually disavows William Shakespeare as author of the Works ascribed to him. If anything, the First Folio is a compelling reason for denying Shakespeare's authorship of it, and for affirming Christopher Marlowe's.

The Folio can no longer be invoked as the stronghold of orthodox belief in William Shakespeare as author. Its reliability as proof of his authorship is too uncertain, too riddled with fraud and misstatement.

We come now to the end of our study.

On the basis of evidence presented, it has been seen that William Shakespeare of Stratford on Avon was never known as a poet or playwright prior to his thirtieth year, or after Christopher Marlowe's reported "assassination"—four months after Marlowe's alleged "decease"; that the "death" of Marlowe and the literary "birth" of Shakespeare are of the most portentous significance to literature.

Previous to Marlowe's alleged "slaying" (on May 30, 1593), and prior to the sudden emergence of "Shakespeare" as a writer (in September, 1593), all that is known of the London actor and businessman is that he was: (1) baptized in 1564; (2) married in 1582; and (3) was the father of three children by 1585, when he was in his twenty-first year.

The interlude between 1585 and 1593 comprises the "lost years," since not a wisp of information on William Shakespeare's life on earth during that time has come to us. Not a jot of evidence about his schooling can be produced.

Testimony has been presented showing that the only reason for ascribing authorship to William Shakespeare at all is that his name appeared in the title pages of nine First Quarto dramas. But it has been shown that the name "William Shakespeare," or the initials "W.S.," appeared in eight rejected First Quarto dramas also. (*Pericles* is the exception.) It is untenable, therefore, to accept "title-page evidence" as an indication of authorship.

It has been shown how unreliable is title-page ascription even in the First Folio.

Objectivity has never governed "William Shakespeare's" acceptance. The arguments of the defense always rise from the premise that he—the London actor—had written the Works in the first place and proceeds from that point onward. Thus, the major premise begins where it should in fact end.

On the other hand, Christopher Marlowe's qualifications for authorship are stunning. They rise from the power of inevitability. Because of his unusual youthful talents, he was awarded a scholarship to King's (Grammar) School and another one to Cambridge University, where he earned the highest academic conferments in Elizabethan England—a Bachelor's and a Master's degree.

At twenty-one or thereabout, while at Corpus Christi College, he wrote *Tamburlaine*—a drama which set the verse-mold for later plays known as "William Shakespeare's." Christopher Marlowe's writing contemporaries—during his "lifetime," or up to his alleged "death" at age 29—eulogized him as the most famous dramatist of the age. As a poet-dramatist he is, therefore, established.

Young Marlowe secured the patronage of an Elizabethan courtier, Sir Thomas Walsingham, and mingled with the brilliant minds of the day. His searching mind forced him to rationalize Scripture, an effort, in those days, akin to atheism and heresy, a crime punishable by burning at the stake. Marlowe voiced his "blasphemies" publicly. The Privy Council kept him under quiet surveillance. When the time came to strike, the government—records attest—arrested him at the home of his patron, May 18, 1593.

Twelve days later—on May 30, 1593—while free under "indemnified" bail, he is "slain" at Deptford. The murderer, Ingram Frizer, and his two accomplices were known employees of Sir Thomas Walsingham. A few weeks later Frizer, the murderer, was given his freedom on the vague plea of self-defense. Marlowe, thereafter, is officially "dead." His crimes of atheism and heresy, and perhaps treason, are wiped away.

Every bit of evidence surrounding the case points to Christopher Marlowe's reported "death" as having been concocted in order to save him from execution.

That someone was killed at Deptford—and that this unknown victim was falsely affirmed to have been Marlowe, our poet—cannot be doubted. William Shakespeare, the London actor, then in his thirtieth year, had not appeared on the scene.

The Coroner's Report detailing Marlowe's "murder" has been rejected, even by conservative scholars.

Four months after the alleged "assassination" of Marlowe (in September, 1593) the name "William Shakespeare" appears before the world for the very first time—also for the very first time as a writer—with a poem, *Venus and Adonis*. This poem bears such an astonishing stylistic resemblance to Marlowe's poem, *Hero and Leander*, that conservative students state that the same hand might well have written both.

Plays attributed to "William Shakespeare" subsequently appear in London which bear a still more striking stylistic resemblance to all the known plays by Marlowe. This "resemblance" is so compelling that orthodox upholders of William Shakespeare's authorship are forced to admit that Christopher Marlowe must have written, in whole or in part, anywhere from three to twenty of the dramas known as "Shakespeare's"!

The *Sonnets* of "Shakespeare," as we have seen, reveal Marlowe's despair.

It has also been seen that in one of the most objectively scientific analyses of literary style ever attempted, Dr. T. C. Mendenhall concluded:

> It was in the counting and plotting of the plays of Christopher Marlowe that something akin to a sensation was produced. . . . In the characteristic curve of his plays Christopher Marlowe agrees with Shakespeare as well as Shakespeare agrees with himself.

Here, then, is the summary—the general aspects of the Marlowe-Shakespeare imposture.

I close this book with a fitting quotation from *Much Ado About Nothing*:

Ursula (to Antonio, who is masked):
> Come, come; do you think I do not know
> you by your excellent wit? Can virtue hide
> itself? Go to, . . . you are he: graces will appear.

Parallelisms

MARLOWE	SHAKESPEARE

Tamburlaine:
   The glory of this happy day is
   yours.

Julius Caesar:
   To part the glories of this happy
   day.

Tamburlaine:
   Ah, Shepherd, pity my distressed
   plight.

Titus Andronicus:
   Comfort his distressed plight.

Tamburlaine:
   And angels dive into the pools of
   hell.

Titus Andronicus:
   I'll dive into the burning lake
   below.

Jew of Malta (end of play):
   . . . for come all the world
   To rescue thee, so will we guard
   us now,
   As sooner they shall drink the
   ocean dry
   Than conquer Malta, or endanger
   us.

King John (end of play):
   Come the three corners of the
   world in arms,
   An we shall shock them. Nought
   shall make us rue,
   If England to itself do rest but
   true.

Jew of Malta:
   These arms of mine shall be thy
   Sepulchure.

Henry VI, Part II:
   These arms of mine shall be thy
   winding sheet;
   My heart, sweet boy, shall be thy
   sepulchure.

Massacre of Paris:
   Yet Caesar shall go forth.
   Thus Caesar did go forth, and
   thus he died.

Julius Caesar:
   Caesar shall go forth.
   Yet Caesar shall go forth.

Elegies (Marlowe's translation of
   Ovid):
   The Moon sleeps with Endymion
   every day.

Merchant of Venice:
   Peace, ho! the Moon sleeps with
   Endymion.

MARLOWE	*SHAKESPEARE*
Tamburlaine: Holla, ye pampered Jades of Asia. What, can ye draw but twenty miles a day?	*Henry IV, Part II*: And hollow pampered jades of Asia, Which cannot go but thirty miles a day.
Tamburlaine: To note me emperor of the three-fold world.	*Julius Caesar*: The three-fold world divided.
Tamburlaine: O, Samarcanda, where I breathed first . . .	*Julius Caesar*: This day I breathed first.
Passionate Shepherd to his Love (Marlowe's poem): By shallow rivers, to whose falls Melodious birds sing madrigals. And I will make thee beds of roses, And a thousand fragrant posies.	*Merry Wives of Windsor*: To shallow rivers, to whose falls Melodious birds sing madrigals: There will we make our beds of roses And a thousand fragrant posies.
Massacre of Paris: Stand close, he is coming. I know him by his voice.	*Julius Caesar*: Casca: Stand close awhile, for he comes in haste. Cassius: Tiz Cinna. I do know him by his gait.
Edward II: Weep not for Mortimer That scorns the world and as a traveller Goes to discover countries yet unknown.	*Hamlet*: The undiscovered country from whose bourn No traveller returns.
Dr. Faustus: Was this the face that launched a thousand ships?	*Troilus and Cressida*: She is a pearl, whose price hath launched above a thousand ships.

MARLOWE	SHAKESPEARE
Edward II:	*Julius Caesar*:
Pembroke: Fear not; the Queen's words cannot alter him.	Look, how he makes to Caesar; mark him.
Warwick: No? Do but mark how earnestly she pleads.	Popilius Lena speaks not of our purposes;
Lancaster: And see how coldly his looks make denial.	For, look, he smiles and Caesar doth not change.
Warwick: She smiles. Now, for my life, his mind is changed.	
Dr. Faustus:	*Merry Wives of Windsor*:
I was no sooner in the middle of the pond, but my horse vanished away . . .	. . . they threw me off, from behind . . . in a slough of mire; and set spurs away, like three German devils, three Doctor Faustuses.
Tamburlaine:	*Romeo and Juliet*:
. . . on thy shining face,	Read o'er the volume of your Paris' face,
Where Beauty, mother to the muses, sits	And find delight writ there with beauty's pen,
And comments volumes with her ivory pen,	And what obscured in this fair volume lies,
Taking instructions from thy flowing eyes.	Find written in the margent of his eyes.
Dido, Queen of Carthage:	*Hamlet*:
Disdaining, whiskt his sword about	But with the whiff and wind of his fell sword
And with the wind thereof the King fell down.	The unnerved father falls.
	Troilus and Cressida:
	The captive Grecian falls
	Even in the fan and wind of your fair sword.
Jew of Malta:	*Othello*:
Poppy and cold mandrake juice.	Not poppy, nor mandragora
	Nor all the drowsy syrups of the world.

Hero and Leander:
   Who ever loved that loved not at first sight.

As You Like It:
   Who ever loved that loved not at first sight.

Edward II:
   Or if I live, let me forget myself.

Richard II:
   Or that I could forget what I have been,
   Or not remember what I must be now.

Edward II:
   Bishop: My lord—
   King Edward: Call me not lord; away—out of my sight!

Richard II:
   Northumberland: My lord—
   Richard: No lord of thine, thou haught, insulting man.

Hero and Leander:
   And now Leander, fearing to be missed,
   Embraced her suddenly, took leave and kissed.
   Long was he taking leave.

Hamlet:
   He took me by the wrist, and held me hard,

   .   .   .   .   .

   And with his other hand thus o'er his brow,
   He falls to such perusal of my face
   As he would draw it. Long stayed he so.

Dido, Queen of Carthage:
   Did ever men see such a sudden storm,
   Or day so clear so suddenly o'er-cast?

Macbeth:
   So foul and fair a day I have not seen.

Hero and Leander:
   Gentle youth, forbear
   To touch the sacred garments which I wear.

Epitaph (on William Shakespeare's grave at Stratford, said to have been written by William Shakespeare):
   Good friend, for Jesus' sake forbear
   To dig the dust enclosed here.

Hero and Leander:
> And to the seat of Jove itself advance,
> Hermes had slept in hell with ignorance.

Sonnet 78:
> But thou art all my art and dost advance,
> As high as learning my rude ignorance.

Jew of Malta:
> I count religion but a childish toy
> And hold there is no sin but ignorance.

Twelfth Night:
> I say there is no darkness but ignorance.

Dido, Queen of Carthage:
> Then from the navel to the throat at once
> He ripped old Priam.

Macbeth:
> And ne'er shook hands, nor bade farewell to him
> Till he enseamed him from the nave to the chaps,
> And fixed his head upon the battlements.

Edward II:
> King Edward: Who's there? Convey this priest to the tower.
> Bishop: True, true!

Richard II:
> Bolingbroke: Go, some of you, convey him to the tower.
> King Richard: O good!—convey!
> Conveyers are you all!

Edward II:
> How now! Why droops the Earl?

Henry VI, Part II:
> Why droops my lord, like over-ripen'd corn?

Jew of Malta:
> Die, life! Fly, soul!
> Tongue, curse thy fill and die!

Timon of Athens:
> Here lies a wretched corpse, of wretched soul bereft;
> Seek not my name; a plague consume you wicked caitiffs left.
> Here lie I, Timon, who, alive all living men did hate.
> Pass by, and curse thy fill; but pass and stay not here thy gait.

207

MARLOWE	SHAKESPEARE

Tamburlaine:
  Black is the beauty of the brightest day.

Love's Labour's Lost:
  That I may swear beauty doth beauty lack,
  No face is fair that is not full so black.

Jew of Malta:
  Now, gentle Ithinore, lie in my lap.

Hamlet:
  Lady, shall I lie in your lap?

Jew of Malta:
  . . . in Ancona once

  .   .   .   .   .

  . . . set it down.

Othello:
  . . . Set you down this;
  . . . in Aleppo once.

Dido, Queen of Carthage:
  In vain, my love, thou spendest thy fainting breath;
  If words might move me, I were overcome.

Julius Caesar:
  I could be well moved if I were as you,
  If I could pray to move, prayers would move me.

Dido, Queen of Carthage (Dido, to her lover):
  . . . if thou wilt stay,
  Leap in mine arms.

Romeo and Juliet (Juliet, to her lover):
  . . . and Romeo
  Leap to these arms . . .

Jew of Malta:
  What? Bring you Scripture to confirm your wrongs?

Merchant of Venice:
  The devil can cite Scripture for his purpose.

Hero and Leander (alluding to Hero's breasts):
  For though the rising ivory mount he scaled,
  Which is with azure circling lines empaled,
  Much like a globe . . . may I term this.

  .   .   .   .   .

  Wherein Leander on her quivering breast . . .

Rape of Lucrece:
  Her breasts, like ivory globes circled with blue
  A pair of maiden worlds unconquered.

Elegies (Marlowe's translation of Ovid):
Let base conceited wits admire vile things,
Fair Phoebus lead me to the Muses' springs.

Timon of Athens:
What viler thing upon the earth than friends
Who can bring noblest minds to basest ends.

Edward II:
Stand not on titles, but obey . . .

Macbeth (Lady Macbeth, to seated Lords):
Stand not upon the order of going,
But go at once.

Edward II:
To die, sweet Spencer, therefore live we all:
Spencer, all live to die.

Julius Caesar:
That we shall die, we know; 'tis but the time,
And drawing days out, that men stand upon.

Edward II (King Edward about his deposition):
Must! It is somewhat hard, when Kings must go!

Richard II (King Richard about his deposition):
What must the King do now? Must he submit?
. . . must he be deposed?

Jew of Malta:
These are the blessings promised to the Jews
And herein was old Abrahams happiness.

Merchant of Venice (referring to Jacob and Abraham):
This was a way to thrive, and he [i.e., Jacob] was blest;
And thrift is blessing, if men steal it not.

Edward II:
Shape we our course to Ireland, there to breathe.

Richard II:
. . . To-morrow next
We will for Ireland; and 'tis time, I trow.

Edward II:
Feared am I more than loved— let me be feared,
And when I frown, make all the court look pale.

Richard II:
To monarchize, be feared, and kill with looks.

Cymbeline:
Fear no more the frown of the great.

MARLOWE	SHAKESPEARE

Jew of Malta:
    And every moon made some or
    other mad.

Othello:
    It is the very error of the moon;
    She comes more nearer than she
      was wont
    And makes men mad.

Edward II:
    Gallop apace, bright Phoebus,
      through the sky,
    And dusky night, in rusty iron
      car,
    Between you both shorten the
      time, I pray,
    That I may see that most desired
      day.

Romeo and Juliet:
    Gallop apace, you fiery footed
      steeds,
    Towards Phoebus lodging; such a
      waggoner
    As Phaeton would whip you to
      the west,
    And bring in cloudy night imme-
      diately.

Jew of Malta (Barabas to his daugh-
    ter):
    O my girl, my fortune, my felic-
      ity;
    O girl, O gold, O beauty, O my
      bliss!

Merchant of Venice (Shylock to his
    daughter):
    My daughter! O my ducats! My
      daughter!
    Fled with a Christian! O my
      Christian ducats!
    Justice! The law! My ducats and
      my daughter!

Edward II:
    I arrest you of high treason.

Henry VIII:
    I arrest thee of high treason.

Edward II:
    And rather bathe thy sword in
    subjects blood.

Julius Caesar:
    And let us bathe our hands in
      Caesar's blood
    Up to the elbows, and besmear
      our swords.

Edward II:
    Remember thee, fellow! what
    else?

Hamlet:
    . . . O, earth!
    . . . what else?
    . . . Remember thee!

Edward II:
    Rain showers of vengeance on my
    cursed head.

Henry VI, Part II:
    Throw in the frozen bosoms of
      our part
    Hot coals of vengeance.

Dr. Faustus:
    Was this the face that launched a
       thousand ships?

Richard II:
    Was this the face that faced so
       many follies?
    . . . was this the face
    That every day under his . . .
    . . . was this the face
    That like the sun . . .

Tamburlaine (addressing dead Zeno-
    crate, his love):
    Now, eyes, enjoy your latest [i.e.,
    last] benefit.

Romeo and Juliet (Romeo address-
    ing dead Juliet, his love):
    Eyes, look your last!

Tamburlaine:
    And in this sweet and curious
       harmony,
    The God that tunes this music
       to our souls . . .

Titus Andronicus:
    Or had he heard the heavenly
       harmony
    Which that sweet tongue hath
       made.

Edward II:
    Earth, melt to air!

Antony and Cleopatra:
    . . . The crown of the earth doth
       melt!

Tamburlaine:
    Blush, blush, fair city.

Macbeth:
    Bleed, bleed, poor country.

Jew of Malta:
    You have my goods, my money,
       and my wealth,
    My ships, my store, and all that
       I enjoyed;
    And having all, you can request
       no more;
    Unless your unrelenting flinty
       hearts
    Suppress all pity in your stony
       breasts,
    And now shall move you to be-
       reave my life.

Merchant of Venice:
    Nay, take my life and all; pardon
       not that.
    You take my house when you do
       take the prop
    That doth sustain my house; you
       take my life
    When you do take the means
       whereby I live.

Tamburlaine:
That flies with fury swifter than our thoughts.

Hamlet:
. . . with wings as swift
As meditation or the thoughts of love.

Love's Labour's Lost:
But love . . .
Courses as swift as thought.

Romeo and Juliet:
. . . love's heralds should be thoughts,
Which ten times faster glide through the sun's beams.

Tamburlaine:
Which makes me valiant, proud, ambitious.

Julius Caesar:
As he was valiant, I honour him,
But as he was ambitious, I slew him.

Jew of Malta:
He that denies to pay shall straight become a Christian.

Merchant of Venice:
. . . that, for this favour,
He presently become a Christian.

Tamburlaine:
For earth and all this airy region
. . .

Romeo and Juliet:
Would through the airy region stream so bright.

Hero and Leander:
. . . she, wanting no excuse to feed him with delays . . .

Titus Andronicus:
He doth me double wrong to feed me with delays.

Edward II:
There is a point, to which men aspire,
They tumble headlong down: that point I touched.

Julius Caesar:
There is a tide in the affairs of men,
Which, taken at the flood, leads on to fortune.

Elegies (Marlowe's translation of Ovid):
Hates any man the thing he would not kill?

Merchant of Venice:
Whom we fear, we wish to perish.

MARLOWE	SHAKESPEARE
Jew of Malta: Infinite riches in a little room.	*As You Like It*: A great reckoning in a little room.
Tamburlaine: Meet, heaven and earth, and here let all things end.	*Romeo and Juliet*: Vile earth, to earth resign, End motion here.
Dr. Faustus: You stars, that reigned at my nativity . . .	*Henry IV, Part I*: At my nativity The front of heaven was full of fiery shapes.
Dr. Faustus: Ugly hell, gape not!	*Hamlet*: . . . though hell itself should gape . . .
Jew of Malta (Barabas, telling of indignities suffered for being a Jew): I learned in Florence how to kiss my hand, Heave up my shoulders when they call me dog, And duck as low as any barefoot friar.	*Merchant of Venice* (Shylock, telling of indignities suffered for being a Jew): Still have I borne it with patient shrug; For sufferance is the badge of all our tribe. You call me disbeliever, cutthroat dog . . .
Edward II: Wet with my tears, and dried again with my sighs.	*Venus and Adonis*: She with her tears Doth quench the maiden burning of his cheeks; Then with windy sighs and golden hairs To fan and blow them dry again she seeks.
Hero and Leander (published in 1598): Rose-cheek'd Adonis . . . Thither resorted . . . a wandering guest To meet their loves.	*Venus and Adonis* (published in 1593): Even as the sun . . . Had taken . . . leave . . . Rose-cheek'd Adonis hied him to the chase.

Timon of Athens:
    Bring down
    Rose-cheek'd youth
    To the tub-fast . . .

Tamburlaine:
    Mingled with coral and with
    orient pearl.

Antony and Cleopatra:
    He kiss'd—the last of many
    doubled kisses—
    This orient pearl.

Midsummer Night's Dream:
    Like round and orient pearl.

Richard III:
    The liquid drops of tears that
    you have shed
    Shall come again, transformed to
    orient pearl.

Tamburlaine:
    The golden ball of Heaven's
    eternal fire . . .

Hamlet:
    This majestical roof fretted with
    golden fire . . .

Tamburlaine:
    For there sits Death, there sits
    imperious Death,
    Keeping his circuit by the slicing
    edge.

Richard II:
    . . . within the hollow crown
    That rounds the mortal temples
    of a king,
    Keeps Death his court and there
    the antic sits,
    Scoffing his state and grinning at
    his pomp.

Tamburlaine:
    Before the moon renew her bor-
    rowed light.

Hamlet:
    Thirty dozen moons with bor-
    rowed sheen . . .

Tamburlaine:
    Fall, stars, that govern his nativ-
    ity . . .

King Lear:
    My nativity was under Ursa
    Major.

Tamburlaine:
    And since this earth dimmed with
    thy brinish tears . . .

Henry VI, Part III:
    To hear and see her plaints, her
    brinish tears . . .

MARLOWE	SHAKESPEARE
Tamburlaine: That, being concocted, turns to crimson blood.	*Henry V:* I will fetch thy rim out at thy throat In drops of crimson blood.
Tamburlaine (mad scene of Zabina): Make ready my coach . . .	*Hamlet* (mad scene of Ophelia): Come, my coach! . . .
Tamburlaine (exacting a love pledge): May never such a change transform my love.	*Hamlet* (exacting a love pledge): And never come mischance between us twain.
Tamburlaine: In frame of which Nature hath showed more skill.	*Merchant of Venice:* Nature hath framed strange fellows in her time. *Pericles:* When nature framed this piece she meant thee a good turn. *Much Ado About Nothing:* Nature never framed a woman's heart Of prouder stuff.
Tamburlaine: Which with thy beauty thou was't wont to light.	*Romeo and Juliet:* . . . her beauty makes This vault a feasting presence of light.
Tamburlaine: Spending my life in sweet discourse of love.	*Romeo and Juliet* (Romeo, to his love): All these woes shall serve for sweet discourses in our time to come.
Hero and Leander: Hero . . . fell down and fainted. He kissed her, and breathed life into her lips.	*Venus and Adonis:* . . . she [Venus] lies as she were slain, Till his breath breatheth life in her again.

Tamburlaine:

> A greater lamp than the bright eye of heaven,
> From whence the stars do borrow all their light.

Timon of Athens:

> . . . but then renew I could not like the moon,
> There were no suns to borrow of.

Tamburlaine:

> Ah, cruel brat, sprung from a tyrant's loins!

Henry VI, Part III:

> O, tiger's heart, wrapped in a woman's hide!

Romeo and Juliet:

> O serpent heart, hid with a flowering face!

Hero and Leander:

> Some swore he was a maid in man's attire.

Venus and Adonis:

> Stain to all nymphs, more lovely than a man.

Tamburlaine:

> Until my soul, dissevered from this flesh,
> Shall mount the milk-white way.

Richard II:

> Mount, mount, my soul! thy seat is up on high,
> Whilst my gross flesh . . .

Tamburlaine:

> 'Tis not thy bloody tents can make me yield,
> Nor yet thyself, the anger of the Highest,
> For though thy cannon shook the city walls,
> My heart did never quake, or courage faint.

Hamlet:

> 'Tis not alone my inky cloak, good mother,
> Nor customary suits of solemn black,
> . . . . .
> For they are actions that a man might play;
> But I have that within which passeth show.

Hero and Leander:

> . . . leapt into the water for a kiss
> Of his own shadow.

Venus and Adonis:

> Died to kiss his shadow in the brook.

Tamburlaine:

> Were full of comets and of blazing stars.

Julius Caesar:

> . . . there are no comets seen;
> The heavens themselves blaze forth.

MARLOWE	SHAKESPEARE

Tamburlaine:
. . . underneath the element of fire.

Antony and Cleopatra:
I am fire and air; my other elements . . .

Jew of Malta:
But stay! What star shines yonder in the East?
The lodestar of my life, if Abigail.

Romeo and Juliet:
But soft! What light through yonder window breaks?
It is the East, and Juliet is the sun!

Hero and Leander:
Love is too full of faith, too credulous,
With folly and false hope deluding us.

Venus and Adonis:
O hard-believing love, how strange it seems
Not to believe, and yet too credulous.

Jew of Malta:
A fair young maid, scarce fourteen years of age,
The sweetest flower in Cytherea's field.

Romeo and Juliet (Juliet, also age 14):
Death lies on her like an untimely frost,
Upon the sweetest flower of all the field.

Hero and Leander:
Hero . . . fell down and fainted.
He kissed her, and breathed life into her lips.

Romeo and Juliet:
I dreamt my lady came and found me dead . . .
And breathed such life with kisses in my lips.

Jew of Malta:
For when their hideous force environed Rhodes.

Romeo and Juliet:
Environed with all those hideous fears.

Elegies (Marlowe's translation of Ovid):
. . . as might make
Wrath-kindled Jove away his thunder shake.

Richard II:
Wrath-kindled gentlemen, be ruled by me.

Hero and Leander:
> . . . then treasure is abused,
> When misers keep it; being put
>   to loan,
> In time it will return us two
>   for one.

Venus and Adonis:
> But gold that's put to use more
>   gold begets.

Tamburlaine:
> Nature doth strive with Fortune
>   and his stars
> To make him famous.

King John:
> Nature and Fortune joined to
>   make thee great.

Hero and Leander:
> For every street like to a firma-
>   ment,
> Glistered with breathing stars,
>   who, where they went,
> Frightened the melancholy earth,
>   which deemed
> Eternal heaven to burn.

Romeo and Juliet:
> Earth-treading stars that make
>   dark heaven light.

Hero and Leander (Leander, wooing Hero to unchastity):
> The richest corn dies, if it be not
>   reaped,
> Beauty alone is lost, too warily
>   kept.

Venus and Adonis (Venus, wooing
Adonis to unchastity):
> Thy unused beauty must be
>   tombed with thee.

Hamlet (Laertes, exhorting Ophelia
—his sister—to chastity):
> The chariest maid is prodigal
>   enough
> If she unmask her beauty to the
>   moon.

> .   .   .   .

> Be wary then; best safety lies in
>   fear.

Tamburlaine:
> Still climbing after knowledge in-
>   finite.

Love's Labour's Lost:
> Still climbing trees in the Hes-
>   perides?

MARLOWE	SHAKESPEARE
Hero and Leander (Leander, wooing Hero to propagation): One is no number, maids are nothing then, Without the sweet society of men.	*Sonnet 8* (exhorting the theme's subject to propagation): Thou, single, wilt prove none.
Edward II (of Queen Isabel): Sits wringing of her hands, and beats her breast!	*Richard III*: Why do you wring your hands, and beat your breast?
	Hamlet (of Queen Gertrude): Leave wringing of your hands.
Edward II: The haughty Dane commands the narrow street.	*Henry VI, Part III*: Stern Falconbridge commands the narrow seas.
Hero and Leander: Thence flew Love's arrow with the golden head.	*Venus and Adonis*: Love's golden arrow at him should have fled.
Edward II: To wretched men, death is felicity.	*Othello*: I'ld have thee live; For, in my sense, 'tis happiness to die.
Edward II: Or whilst one is asleep, to take a quill And blow a little powder in his ears, Or open his mouth and pour quicksilver down.	*Hamlet* (how Hamlet's father met his death): Sleeping within mine orchard, My custom always in the afternoon, Upon my secure hour thy uncle stole With juice of cursed hebenon in a vial And in the porches of mine ears did pour The leperous distillment, ... That, swift as quicksilver . . .

Edward II:
    These looks of thine can harbor naught but death.

King John:
    For I do see the cruel pangs of death
    Right in thine eye.

Edward II:
    For he's a lamb, encompassed by wolves.

Romeo and Juliet:
    Dove-feathered raven! wolfish-ravening lamb.

Edward II:
    Inhuman creatures!—nursed with Tiger's milk.

Henry VI, Part III:
    O Tiger's heart, wrapped in a woman's hide!

Edward II (at being deposed):
    Here, take my crown; the life of Edward too!

Richard II (at being deposed):
    . . . Here, cousin, seize the crown!

Hero and Leander:
    And with intestine broils the world destroy.

Henry IV, Part I:
    And breathe short-winded accents of new broils

      .   .   .   .   .

    Did lately meet in the intestine shock,
    And furious close of civil butchery.

Hero and Leander:
    And made confusion run through her streets amazed.

Julius Caesar:
    Fled to his house amazed:
    Men, wives, and children stare, cry out, and run,
    As if it were doomsday.

Hero and Leander:
    Dear place, I kiss thee, and do welcome thee!

Richard II:
    Dear earth, I do salute thee with my hand!

Hero and Leander:
    And have an antic face to laugh within.

Hamlet:
    As I perchance hereafter shall think meet
    To put an antic disposition on.

Tamburlaine:
  Whose darts do pierce the centre
  of my soul.

Sonnet 146:
  Poor soul, the centre of my sinful earth.

Tamburlaine:
  The sun, unable to sustain the
  sight,
  Shall hide his head.

Romeo and Juliet:
  The sun for sorrow will not show
  his head.

Tamburlaine:
  Flying dragons, lightning, fearful
  thunderclaps.
  Singe these fair plains!

King Lear:
  Vaunt couriers of oak-cleaving
  thunderbolts,
  Singe my white head!

Tamburlaine:
  View me, thy father,
  And see him lance his flesh to
  teach you all.

Julius Caesar:
  I have made strong proof of my
  constancy
  Giving myself a voluntary wound
  Here in the thigh.

Hero and Leander:
  And half the world upon breathed
  darkness forth.

Macbeth:
  Now o'er the one half world
  nature seems dead.

Tamburlaine:
  Go thou frowning forth; but come
  thou smiling home,
  As did Paris with the Grecian
  dame.

Henry VI, Part I:
  . . . and thus he goes,
  As did the youthful Paris once to
  Greece.

Tamburlaine:
  Whose ransom made them march
  in coats of gold.

Julius Caesar:
  Whose ransoms did the general
  coffers fill.

Tamburlaine:
  A pearl, more worth than all the
  world.

Othello:
  . . . threw a pearl away
  Richer than all his tribe.

Tamburlaine:
>Then *haste,* Corsoe, to be king alone,
>*That* I, with these my friends and all my men,
>*May* triumph in our long expected fate.

Hamlet:
>*Haste* me to know it, *that* I, with wings as swift
>As meditation or the thoughts of love,
>*May* sweep to my revenge.

Tamburlaine:
>Our souls, whose faculties can comprehend
>The wondrous architecture of the world,
>And measure every wandering planet's course,
>Still climbing after knowledge infinite,
>And always moving as the restless spheres,
>Will us to wear ourselves and never rest
>Until we reach the ripest fruit of all.

Hamlet:
>. . . what a piece of work is a man! How noble in reason! how infinite in faculty! in form and moving how express and admirable! in action how like an angel; in apprehension how like a god! the beauty of the world! the paragon of animals! And yet, to me, what is this quintessence of dust?

Tamburlaine:
>To cast up hills against the face of heaven.

Hamlet:
>And bowl the round knave down the hill of heaven.

Tamburlaine:
>Tell him thy lord . .
> . . . . .
>Wills and commands, for say not I entreat.

Julius Caesar:
>And tell them I will not come today:
>Cannot is false; and that I dare not, falser:
>I will not come today; tell them so, Decius.

Tamburlaine (rapturously about his love):
>Zenocrate, the loveliest maid alive . . .
> . . . . .
>Whose eyes are brighter than the lamps of heaven.

Romeo and Juliet (rapturously about his love):
>Two of the fairest stars [i.e., eyes] in all the heaven . . .
> . . . . .
>The brightness of those cheeks would shame those stars,
>As daylight doth a lamp.

MARLOWE	SHAKESPEARE
Tamburlaine: The sun, unable to sustain the sight, Shall hide his head.	*Timon of Athens*: Sun, hide thy beams.
Tamburlaine: When Phoebus, leaping from the hemisphere, Descendeth downward to the Antipodes.	*Richard II*: . . . when the searching eye of heaven is hid, Behind the globe that lights the lower world, ... Whilst we were wandering with the Antipodes.
Tamburlaine: That Jove shall send his winged messenger . . .	*Romeo and Juliet*: . . . being o'er my head As is a winged messenger of heaven.
Tamburlaine: Most great and puissant Monarch of the earth.	*Julius Caesar*: Most high, most mighty and most puissant Caesar.
Tamburlaine: And might, if my extremes had full events, Make me the ghastly counterfeit of death.	*Macbeth*: Shake off this downy sleep, death's counterfeit, And look on death itself.
Dr. Faustus: Was this the face that launched a thousand ships?	*All's Well That Ends Well*: Was this fair face the cause, quoth she, Why the Grecians sacked Troy?
Dr. Faustus: Cut is the branch that might have grown full straight, And burned is Apollo's laurel bough.	*Antony and Cleopatra*: O, withered is the garland of the war, The soldiers pole is fallen!
Massacre of Paris: . . . breakers of the peace!	*Romeo and Juliet*: . . . disturbers of the peace!

MARLOWE	SHAKESPEARE
Jew of Malta (Barabas, being dragged to death): Die, life! Fly, soul! Tongue, curse thy fill and die!	*Timon of Athens* (Timon's epitaphic curse to the living): Pass by, and curse thy fill!
Edward II: A lofty cedar-tree, fair flourishing, On whose top-branches kingly eagles perch.	*Henry VI, Part III*: Thus yields the cedar to the axe's edge, Whose arms gave shelter to the princely eagle. *Richard III*: . . . where eagles dare not perch.
Edward II: You must be proud, bold, pleasant, resolute, And now and then stab . . .	*Macbeth*: Be bloody, bold and resolute.
Edward II (fantastic dress allusion): . . . and, in his Tuscan cap, A jewel of more value . . .	*Romeo and Juliet* (fantastic dress allusion): Like a rich jewel in an Ethiope's ear.
Edward II (urging the King to bravery): . . . shall the crowing of these cockerels Affright a lion? Edward, unfold thy paws.	*Richard II* (urging the King to bravery): The lion dying thrusteth forth his paw And wounds the earth . . .
Edward II: My swelling heart for very anger breaks!	*Titus Andronicus*: The venomous malice of my swelling heart.
Tamburlaine: Meet, heaven and earth.	*Romeo and Juliet*: Since . . . heaven and earth . . . do meet.
Edward II: And let these tears, distilling from mine eyes . . .	*Romeo and Juliet*: With tears distilled by moans . . .

Dido, Queen of Carthage (abjuring her lover—calling him liar):
Thy mother was no Goddess, perjured man,

. . . . .

But thou art sprung from Scythian Caucasus,
And Tigers of Hyrcania gave thee suck;

. . . . .

O Serpent that came creeping from the shore!

Romeo and Juliet (abjuring her lover—calling him liar):
O Serpent heart, hid with a flowering face!
Did ever dragon keep so fair a cave?
. . . O that deceit should dwell
In such a gorgeous palace.

Henry VI, Part III:
O Tiger's heart, wrapped in a woman's hide!

Edward II:
O day, the last of all my bliss on earth!
Centre of all misfortune!

Sonnet 146:
Poor soul, the centre of my sinful earth!

Jew of Malta:
My sinful soul . . .

Dido, Queen of Carthage:
And Tigers of Hyrcania gave thee suck;
O serpent that came creeping from the shore!

Henry VI, Part III:
You are more inhuman, more inexorable,
O ten times more than Tigers of Hyrcania.

Macbeth:
Approach thou like . . .
. . . the Hyrcan Tiger . . .

Tamburlaine:
Vast Grantland, compassed with the frozen sea.

Romeo and Juliet:
That far shore, washed with the farthest sea.

Hero and Leander:
. . . they took delight
To play upon those hands, they were so white.

Romeo and Juliet:
. . . they may seize
On the white wonder of dear Juliet's hands.

Dido, Queen of Carthage:
Dry with grief . . .

Romeo and Juliet:
. . . dry sorrow drinks our blood.

Tamburlaine:
  And sorrow stops the passage of
  my speech.

Henry VI, Part III:
  . . . my father's blood hath
  Stopped the passage where thy
  words should enter.

Edward II:
  With slaughtered priests make
  Tibers channel swell,
  And banks raised higher with
  their sepulchres!

Julius Caesar:
  An universal shout . . .
  That Tiber trembled under-
  neath her banks.

Cymbeline:
  . . . and Cydus swelled above the
  banks.

Edward II:
  Can kingly lions fawn on creeping ants?

Henry VI, Part III:
  When the lion fawns upon the
  man . . .

Edward II:
  There's none here but would run
  his horse to death.

Henry VI, Part III:
  That beggars mounted run their
  horse to death.

Edward II:
  My heart is as an anvil unto
  sorrow
  Which beats upon it like the
  Cyclops' hammers.

Richard II:
  . . . the sound that tells what
  hour it is,
  Are clamorous groans that strike
  upon my heart,
  Which is the bell.

Hamlet:
  And never did the Cyclops' hammers fall.

Tamburlaine (to his love):
  Fair is too foul an epithet for
  thee!

Sonnet 137:
  To put fair truth upon so foul a
  face.

Tamburlaine:
  Like summers vapours vanished
  by the sun.

Comedy of Errors:
  The sun, gazing upon the earth,
  Dispersed those vapours.

MARLOWE	SHAKESPEARE
Edward II (fantastic dress allusion): Whose proud fantastic liveries make such show.	*Hamlet* (fantastic dress allusion): There with fantastic garlands did she come Of crow-flowers, nettles . . .
Edward II: And, as gross vapours perish by the sun . . .	*Romeo and Juliet*: Now, ere the sun advance his burning eye The day to cheer and nights dank dew to dry.
Edward II: Is all my hope turned to this hell of grief?	*Julius Caesar*: Are all thy conquests . . . Shrunk to this little measure?
Tamburlaine: Have make the waters swell above the banks.	*Cymbeline*: And Cydnus swelled above the banks.
Tamburlaine: The monster that hath drunk a sea of blood, And yet gapes still more to quench his thirst.	*Macbeth*: That which hath made them drunk hath made me bold; What hath quenched them hath given me fire.
Dr. Faustus: Sweet Helen, make me immortal with a kiss. Her lips suck forth my soul . . .	*Romeo and Juliet*: And steal immortal blessing from her lips.
Edward II: Father, this life contemplative is Heaven. O that I might this life in quiet lead!	*Richard III*: 'Tis hard to draw from thence, So sweet is zealous contemplation.
Edward II: In civil broils make kin and countrymen.	*Henry VI, Part I*: Prosper this realm, keep it from civil broils.

Jew of Malta:
  As sooner shall they drink the
  ocean dry.

Richard II:
  The task he undertakes . . .
  Is numbering sands and drinking
  oceans dry.

Tamburlaine:
  Unto the rising of this earthly
  globe;
  Whereas the sun, declining from
  our sight,
  Begins the day with our Antipodes.

Richard II:
  Behind the globe that lights the
  lower world,
  Whilst we were wandering with
  the Antipodes.

Jew of Malta:
  And Barabas, now search this
  secret out:
  Summon thy senses; call thy wits
  together.

Henry V:
  Once more to the breach, dear
  friends, once more:

  .   .   .   .   .

  Stiffen the sinews, summon up
  the blood.

Dr. Faustus:
  O soul! be changed into small
  water-drops.

Richard II:
  O, that I were a mockery king of
  snow,
  To melt myself away in water-
  drops.

Tamburlaine:
  As many circumcized Turks . . .

Othello:
  . . . and a turbaned Turk
  I took by the throat the circumcized dog.

Dido, Queen of Carthage:
  To move unto the measures of
  delight.

Richard II:
  My legs can keep no measure
  with delight.

Massacre of Paris:
  For his oaths are seldom spent in
  vain.

Richard II:
  When words are scarce, they're
  seldom spent in vain.

Tamburlaine:
  And in my blood wash all your
  hands at once.

Julius Caesar:
  . . . let us bathe our hands in
  Caesar's blood.

MARLOWE	SHAKESPEARE

Tamburlaine:
Will make the hair stand upright on your heads.

Hamlet:
And each particular hair to stand on end.

Tamburlaine:
And cause the sun to borrow light of you.

Timon of Athens:
There were no suns to borrow of.

Tamburlaine:
Hell and confusion light upon their heads!

Timon of Athens:
Decrees, observances, customs and laws,

.   .   .   .   .

Decline to your confounding contraries,
And let confusion live!

Tamburlaine:
My mind pressageth fortunate success.

Romeo and Juliet:
My dreams presage some joyful news at hand.

Tamburlaine:
Here is my dagger.

Julius Caesar:
. . . there is my dagger

Tamburlaine:
. . . and laugh to scorn
The former triumphs of our mightiness.

Macbeth:
. . . laugh to scorn
The power of man.

Tamburlaine:
Shaking her silver tresses in the air.

Henry VI, Part I:
Brandish your crystal tresses in the sky.

Tamburlaine (about his seeming cowardice):
But how unseemly is it for my sex,

.   .   .   .   .

My nature, and the terror of my name,
To harbour thoughts effeminate and faint.

Romeo and Juliet (about his seeming cowardice):
. . . O sweet Juliet,
Thy beauty hath made me effeminate,
And in my temper softened valour's steel.

Tamburlaine:
> . . . let us glut our swords,
> That thirst to drink the feeble
> Persian's blood.

Julius Caesar:
> . . . let us bathe our hands in
> Caesar's blood
> Up to the elbows, and besmear
> our swords.

Tamburlaine:
> Yet be not so inconstant in your
> love.

Romeo and Juliet:
> O, swear not by the moon, the
> inconstant moon,
>
> .   .   .   .   .
>
> Lest thy love prove likewise vari-
> able.

Tamburlaine:
> For he that gives him other food
> than this,
> Shall sit by him and starve to
> death himself!

Titus Andronicus:
> There let him starve, and rave,
> and cry for food;
> If any one relieves or pities him,
> For the offence he dies!

Tamburlaine:
> Ye furies that can mask invisible,
> Dive to the bottom of Avernus'
> pool,
> And in your hands bring hellish
> poison up.

Titus Andronicus:
> I'll dive into the burning Lake
> below
> And pull her out of Acheron by
> the heels.

Tamburlaine (in deep remorse):
> That in this terror Tamburlaine
> may live,
> And my pined soul, resolved in
> liquid air,
> May still excruciate his tormented
> thoughts!

Othello (in deep remorse):
> Blow me about in winds! Roast
> me in sulphur!
> Wash me steep-down in liquid
> fire!

Tamburlaine:
> Earth, cast up fountains from
> thy enthrails.

Richard II:
> Dear earth . . .
> Yield stinging nettles to mine
> enemies.

Timon of Athens:
> Earth, yield me roots!

Tamburlaine (about filial duty):
My father and my first betrothed
love
Must fight against my life and
present love.

Othello (about filial duty):
My noble father,
I do perceive here a divided duty.
. . . . .
. . . you are the lord of duty,
. . . but here's my husband.

Tamburlaine:
What god or fiend, or spirit of
the earth,
Or monster turned to manly
shape
. . . . .
Whether from earth, or hell, or
heaven he grow.

Hamlet:
Be thou a spirit of health or goblin damned,
Bring with thee airs from heaven,
or blasts from hell.

Tamburlaine:
Weep, heavens, and vanish into
liquid tears.

Antony and Cleopatra:
Dissolve, thick cloud, and rain,
that I may say
The Gods themselves do weep.

Tamburlaine (beginning of scene):
Black is the beauty of the brightest day!

Henry VI, Part I (beginning of
scene):
Hung be the heavens with black,
yield day to night.

Tamburlaine (speaking of Zenocrate, about to die):
Whose heavenly presence . . .
Gives light to Phoebus and the
fixed stars!

Romeo and Juliet (speaking of dead
Juliet):
A grave? O no, a lantern, slaughtered youth,
For here lies Juliet, and her
beauty makes
This vault a feasting presence
full of light.

Tamburlaine:
Their hair as white as milk and
soft as down,
Which should be like the quills
of porcupines.

Hamlet:
And each particular hair to stand
on end,
Like quills upon the fretful porcupine.

231

MARLOWE	SHAKESPEARE

Tamburlaine (dying):

    Ah, that the deadly pangs I suf-
fer now,

    Would lend an hour's licence to
my tongue.

Hamlet (dying):

    Had I but time—as this fell
sergeant, Death,

    Is strict in his arrest—O, I could
tell you—

Tamburlaine:

    . . . shall we wish for aught

    The world affords in greatest
novelty

    And rest attemptless, faint and
destitute?

Macbeth:

    Wouldst thou have that

    Which thou esteemst the orna-
ment of life

    And live a coward in thine own
esteem . . .?

Dr. Faustus (to Helen):

    Here will I dwell, for heaven be
in these lips,

      .   .   .   .   .

    And none but thou shalt be my
paramour!

Romeo and Juliet:

    . . . shall . . . death . . . keep

    Thee here in the dark to be his
paramour?

    . . . Here, here I will remain!

Tamburlaine (speaking of Zenocrate, his dead wife, lying before him):

    And here will I set up her statue.

Romeo and Juliet (speaking of a
dead wife, Juliet, whose body
lies in view):

    For I will raise her statue in pure
gold.

Tamburlaine:

    Now are those spheres where
Cupid used to sit,

    Wounding the world with wonder.

Hamlet:

    . . . whose praise of sorrow

    Conjures the wandering stars, and
makes them stand

    Like wonder-wounded hearers.